practical gardening

practical gardening

Deena Beverley

p

This is a Parragon Book
This edition published in 2003

Parragon
Queen Street House
4 Queen Street
Bath BA1 1HE, UK
Copyright © Parragon 2002

ISBN: 0-75259-628-4

A CIP data record for this book is available from the British Library.

Created and produced by
Foundry Design and Production.

Acknowledgements
Text: Deena Beverley
Illustrations: Kate Simunek
Special photography: Andrew Newton-Cox

Printed in China

CONTENTS

❀

Introduction 7

❀

Before you begin 9

❀

Caring for your plants 43

❀

Pests and weeds 85

❀

Index 96

INTRODUCTION

❦

Gardening is very hard work, especially if you are creating a new garden from scratch, or completely changing the style of an established garden – but once you have put in all the initial effort, and you can start to appreciate the results, it is extremely rewarding and worthwhile.

✿

Gardening is not always about creating the new, however – it may be that you have just bought your first home with a garden and, although you are delighted and excited, you are suddenly faced with maintaining something about which you have no knowledge.

✿

Whatever your circumstances, there is no doubt that some expert guidance on the many pitfalls and pleasures of gardening is invaluable. It will make all the difference, for example, to know what equipment is available to make the task easier, how to overcome climatic challenges and work with the seasons, how to feed and protect your plants and how to maintain and increase your stock.

✿

Practical Gardening is full of useful information and tips that will take away some of the mystery and inspire you with all the magic of gardening, so that you can work with confidence to keep your garden looking its very best throughout the year.

BEFORE YOU BEGIN

As with many creative tasks, the best results in the garden undoubtedly come from thorough preparation – but how do you go about this?

Understanding the effects of the climate and the type of soil you have to work with is a good start. Digging over the soil, feeding it with the appropriate nutrients and providing extra drainage if necessary are all tasks that need to be completed before you start planting.

There is a whole range of useful equipment to help you, and each piece has a different purpose – this chapter will guide you to selecting the right tool for the job you need to tackle.

If you think that watering the garden is the easy part, you will be surprised to learn that there is a right and a wrong way even for this. And always remember that gardening needs a slow and steady pace – it cannot be rushed.

GARDENING TOOLS AND EQUIPMENT

❧

Care of even the smallest garden requires some specialised tools and equipment. Confronted with the range available at hardware and garden stores, it is easy to be bewildered into inappropriate purchasing, so spend some time considering your needs before venturing to the shops. The range of tools required will depend on the size of your garden and the type of gardening you plan to undertake. For example, a garden with a huge lawn may prompt the purchase of a sit-and-ride mower, while a tiny lawn will have far more modest mowing needs. Similarly, a keen vegetable grower will benefit from a range of cultivation tools, while a topiarist will need special shears.

A BASIC GARDEN TOOL KIT

WHATEVER the size of your garden, quality is of paramount importance when selecting tools – be they for cultivation, digging, pruning or cutting. These tools will be in regular use for many years and it is worth investing in the best quality available. A cheap fork that bends on contact with compacted soil is frustratingly useless and a complete waste of money. It can be galling to spend large sums on basic tools when there are so many other, more immediately exciting temptations on sale in the garden centre, but sturdy, comfortable and effective tools really will turn basic gardening functions into much more pleasurable tasks.

Spades and forks

❀ You will be using spades and forks regularly so it is vital to select models that are comfortable for you to handle. Great demands will be made on both items in terms of lifting and leverage, so look for designs that combine lightness with strength.

❀ Consider the material of the head carefully before purchase. Stainless steel does not rust but is expensive; coated steel blades are more affordable and will last well if kept clean, but beware of inexplicably cheap tools – the coating is likely to be so thin that it will lift away almost immediately.

❀ Non-stick coatings are available, and undoubtedly make cleaning the tool and working the soil easier, but may wear off after lengthy use.

❀ As with all tools, check that all the joints are secure – particularly where the head of the tool meets the shaft, as this joint will be under a lot of pressure in use.

ABOVE: A well-stocked and well-ordered garden shed with neatly stored tools is pleasant and efficient to use.

✿ For optimum strength ensure that the head and neck are moulded from a single piece of metal. Shafts may be of wood or metal, possibly covered with plastic. Both are generally strong. Wooden shafts have the advantage of being easy to replace and warmer to handle in winter than even plastic-coated metal. Ensure that the tines or blades are smooth, for ease of working and cleaning.

✿ Handle shapes differ so don't be afraid to experiment with the varying types – D-, Y- and T-shapes – in the shop, until you arrive at a model that feels right in the hand. The Y-shape, formed by splitting the shaft wood, may not be as strong as the D-shaped hilt.

✿ Although there are various sizes of spade and fork available – for example border (small, sometimes called 'ladies'), medium and digging (generally the largest) – do not feel that you need a whole selection for different tasks. A fork is useful for turning heavy soil, dividing or transplanting plants, spreading mulch, applying manure and lifting root vegetables.

✿ The addition of a tread on a spade makes digging easier, and less hazardous to footwear, but also adds weight and cost, which it may not be necessary to incur if you have only minimal digging requirements. Be guided by the head size, length and weight that feels most workable for your stature and strength.

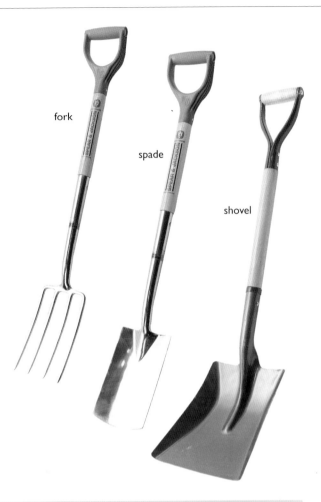

fork

spade

shovel

EARLY GARDENS

THE earliest gardens we have pictures of are Egyptian ones, created over 3,000 years ago. In Egypt the narrow fertile stretch of the Nile is surrounded by desert. The idea of paradise was centred on an enclosed green oasis full of water and fruitfulness. In fact, water became the most important aspect of the garden, both for irrigation and as a symbol of the River of Life. All the irrigated gardens of Persia, Arabia and India developed from these Egyptian gardens. Their influence could be seen in ancient Roman gardens and was brought to medieval Europe by knights returning from the Crusades, and to Spain through the Moorish invasions from North Africa.

The Hanging Gardens of Babylon, built in 605 BC, were different. They consisted of a series of steep terraces planted with trees and shrubs, created by Nebuchadnezzar II for his Persian wife, who was homesick for the green hillsides of her home. They

ABOVE: *This picture of a man and woman ploughing and sowing seed shows the typical boundary of tall trees that lined ancient Egyptian gardens. It comes from a tomb in Thebes, dated about 1200 BC.*

were, basically, the first roof gardens and for many centuries they were considered to be among the Seven Wonders of the World.

Hand forks and trowels

❀ Essentially miniature spades and forks, these tools are used for small-scale jobs like light weeding, cultivating in rock gardens, raised beds and containers, and dividing small bulbs and plants. As before, choose the best quality you can afford, making sure the tool feels comfortable to hold.

❀ Hand forks have either wide and flat, or narrow, round prongs. The flat prongs are more suited to weeding since the weeds are more easily trapped and held between them; the round, narrow prongs are better for cultivating as they pass freely through the earth. A single, flat-pronged hand fork will be adequate for most gardeners.

hand fork
and trowel

Hoes

❀ Hoes are used for weeding around plants and cultivating topsoil. There are several types. The popular 'Dutch' hoe is used like a sharp-bladed spoon to skim along the surface of the soil, loosening weeds, which may then be sliced through. Turned so that the blade is at right angles to the ground, it may also be used to break up and aerate topsoil.

❀ The small, sharp head of the hoe is useful for making seed drills and marking out lines. Swan-neck, or draw hoes, used in a chopping motion for weeding, are less commonly used; other, specialised hoes include onion and triangular hoes.

Garden rakes

❀ A general-purpose cultivation tool, the garden rake can be used with its prongs facing down to break up the surface of the soil and collect stones, leaves and other debris. Inverted, it is used to level the ground. Choose a rake with a head of suitable width for both your own size and the scale of raking job you will most commonly undertake.

❀ Choose shaft length carefully, too. To avoid back strain, you should be able to rake without bending. A 1.5 m (5 ft) shaft suits most people, but taller gardeners may need a longer handle. The strongest rake head is made in a single piece, unlike the cheaper, riveted head with its individual nail-like prongs, which are more liable to distortion and loss. A lawn rake is an entirely different tool (see p. 38).

Gardener's knives

❀ The general-purpose gardener's knife is possibly the most essential garden tool. Use it to open bags of compost, cut twine and cane to length, and for taking cuttings, pruning small plants and deadheading. A plastic or wooden handle is not as cold to handle in winter as a metal one. Choose a carbon-steel blade for longevity, wiping it dry and rubbing it over with an oily rag after use.

❀ Specialist knives include budding and curved pruning knives; multi-purpose knives have several different types of blade folded into one handle.

garden rakes

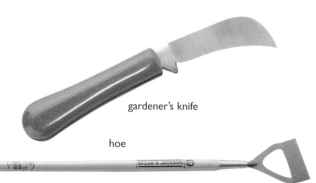

gardener's knife

hoe

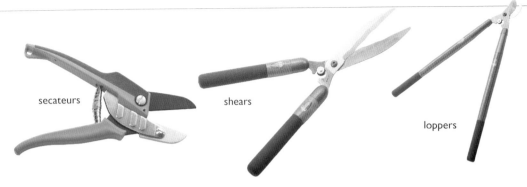

secateurs   shears   loppers

Secateurs

❀ For cutting that is slightly more demanding than deadheading and harvesting, a pair of secateurs is essential. Good ones will cut cleanly and easily through woody stems up to approximately 1 cm ($\frac{1}{2}$ in) in diameter. It is vital that the blades are sharp or you will achieve either a ragged stem, which will encourage disease in the plant, or a crushed stem.

❀ There are a confusing range of secateur types available. As always, your hands are the best guides. Select a pair that suits the hand you use most, since both left- and right-handed pairs are available.

❀ Bypass secateurs are a good, multi-purpose pair. They have a convex upper blade, which cuts in a scissor motion against a narrow, concave lower blade, and are comfortable for general use. If your hand span is small, or you do not have particularly strong hands, opt for ratchet secateurs, which make pruning thicker stems infinitely easier as the ratchet action makes the cut in several small stages, rather than requiring all your strength to make one powerful cut. However, the ratchet action is frustratingly slow if used for general cutting tasks.

❀ Other options include parrot-beak secateurs, which use a scissor action, and anvil secateurs, which have a sharp upper blade that cuts against a flat anvil. All secateurs have a safety catch, which should be easy to operate single handed.

❀ When choosing any pair of secateurs, consider how easy it will be to sharpen or replace the blades. Clean the blades after use to remove dried sap, and rub them with an oily rag.

❀ To use secateurs correctly, always place the stem to be cut well down at the base of the blades. This holds the stem securely, making an accurate cut much simpler to perform. It also preserves blade life as the blades are less likely to be pushed out of alignment.

Shears

❀ Shears are used for topiary, cutting back herbaceous plants and trimming hedges and small areas of long grass. Although some shears have a notch at the base of one blade to facilitate the cutting of the occasional tough stem, shears are best reserved for their specific, light 'hair cutting' work. Use proper pruning tools to tackle heavier stems and branches.

❀ A good pair of shears will be light, strong and comfortable to operate. Check their balance before purchasing, to ensure that the blades are not much heavier than the handles, which makes them tiring to use.

❀ As with all cutting tools, clean and lightly oil after use, and sharpen regularly. Specialist shears, such as topiary shears, are also available.

Loppers, tree pruners and pruning saws

❀ Cutting branches and stems thicker than about 1 cm ($\frac{1}{2}$ in) quickly damages secateurs and shears, and is dealt with most effectively by specialist tools.

❀ Loppers (long-handled pruners) are essentially secateurs with additional leverage and reach, making it easy to cut stems up to about 2.5 cm (1 in) thick and branches that are difficult to reach. Loppers should be well balanced so that you can use them comfortably at full stretch and overhead.

❀ Tree pruners also cut branches up to 2.5 cm (1 in) thick. The cutting device, operated by a lever or cord, is housed at the end of a long pole, sometimes an extending or telescopic one.

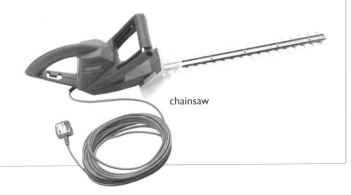

chainsaw

pruning saw

❀ For branches more than 2.5 cm (1 in) thick, use a pruning saw. A general-purpose pruning saw will be sufficient for most needs. Its small blade, usually no more than 46 cm (18 in) long, means that it may be used even in confined spaces.

❀ A Grecian saw has a curved blade, which cuts on the pull stroke only – particularly useful for pruning in a tight area. A small, folding pruning saw is ideal for those with limited storage space and pruning needs. However, it is not as strong and effective as a bow saw, which will cut through even thick branches quickly.

❀ All types should have heat-treated, hard-point teeth, which are tougher and stay sharper for longer than regular saw blades, although they still need regular sharpening to remain fully effective.

OTHER GARDENING EQUIPMENT

IN addition to basic cultivating, digging, pruning and cutting tools, you will need equipment for carrying, such as trugs and buckets, for watering and for propagating, for example a garden sieve, flowerpots, string, plant labels and canes.

Carrying equipment

❀ A folding wheelbarrow is useful in situations where storage space is limited, although not as sturdy as a conventional barrow and its canvas can be damaged by careless handling.

❀ Choose a barrow that is well balanced, where the load is distributed chiefly over the wheel, rather than towards the handles, for good manoeuvrability. Metal barrows are more durable than plastic ones; a galvanised traditional barrow is a good all-round choice for most gardens.

❀ For very heavy loads, or for use on uneven ground, a builder's ball-wheeled barrow cushions the load and is easier to push, but the ball is susceptible to punctures.

❀ Bulky but light materials such as hedge trimmings can be easily collected and transported on ground sheets and in large bags, which can be conveniently folded flat for easy storage. Look for those made of woven mesh plastic material and with sturdy handles, which wear better than ordinary plastic.

Hose and watering can

❀ The humble hose is a vital piece of garden equipment. If not stored neatly on a reel it is vulnerable to kinks and punctures, as well as posing a tripping hazard.

❀ Many variants of hose are available, including the convenient flow-through type which allows water to be run through it even while it is stored on the reel. Always drain a hose fitted to an outside tap and bring it inside for the winter.

hosepipe

wheelbarrow

watering can and rose

LAWN EQUIPMENT

T HE tools you purchase for your lawn will depend on
its size and structure, whether it is sloping or flat, has
intricate shapes to cut around or is a simple rectangle, and
what type of lawn you require – be it a wild meadow or an
elegant, striped bowling green-type lawn. For the former,
which needs trimming only once or twice a year, a sickle
or a power trimmer may be all you need. Your choice of
equipment will also be governed by how much time and
money you have available.

❀ A well-made metal watering can with a detachable rose
will last for years. Always use a separate watering can
for applying weedkiller, path clearer and other noxious
substances that could cause plant damage if allowed to
contaminate clean water. It is worth investing in a
cheap, plastic watering can solely for this purpose.

Kneeling mat

❀ A cushioned kneeling mat is invaluable for gardeners
of all ages and is inexpensive and easy to store.
❀ A more expensive and bulky option is the
kneeling frame, which has the added advantage
of supportive handles that make it easier to
stand up and kneel down.
❀ This sort of frame is an excellent choice for
the elderly, or indeed any gardener with back
problems; used the other way up, it becomes
a handy stool.

Lawnmowers

❀ Scarcely used today, the manual lawnmower is
wonderfully quiet in use and easy to maintain, and
is still a viable option for a small lawn.
❀ Electric or petrol-driven cylinder lawnmowers are
heavy and tiring to use, but produce the clean, close cut
desirable on a luxury lawn. They require good
maintenance and are generally for those who enjoy
spending time and energy on their lawns.
❀ Probably the most well-known power lawnmower
is the electric hover mower, which glides above the
lawn on a cushion of air. It is light, easy and quick
to use but does not cut as closely as a cylinder mower
and is not recommended where a really pristine,
formal finish is required.

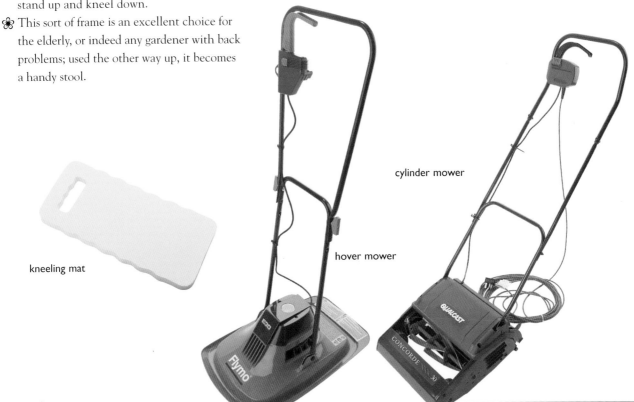

kneeling mat

hover mower

cylinder mower

Lawn edging and maintenance tools

❀ Often overlooked, edging tools add the finishing touch to lawns and are worth investing in.

❀ A lawn edging iron is essential for cutting away any rough edges where the lawn meets the soil of a border. Long-handled lawn edging shears are required for the long, untidy grass at the edges of a lawn.

❀ Power trimmers, driven by electricity or petrol, cut through grass and weeds using a fast-rotating nylon line. They are especially convenient to use in a confined area.

❀ Electric trimmers are cheaper and lighter than the petrol-driven equivalents, but need a power source close by and are not suitable for use on wet grass.

❀ A fan-shaped, spring-tined wire-headed rake is useful for removing lawn moss and leaves and also for aerating the lawn.

Tool care

❀ Regular cleaning and maintenance is essential for prolonging the life of tools. In addition, blunt blades will damage vulnerable plant tissues, and dirty tools simply do not function as well as clean ones. A mud-encrusted spade cannot cut into the soil as effectively as a clean one, making digging even more arduous. Similarly, grit works its way into joints and pivot points, causing moving parts to seize up and preventing blades meeting efficiently.

❀ Clean all tools after use and wipe metal surfaces with an oily rag to protect them against rust.

❀ Wipe electrical tools clean, and dry them thoroughly before storing. Have them serviced regularly – a label on the handle, indicating the date of the last service and a reminder of the next one, is helpful.

SAFETY IN THE GARDEN

THE garden can be a dangerous environment if some basic safety guidelines are not adhered to. Eyes are particularly at risk and safety goggles are advisable for jobs such as hedge trimming and lawn mowing, which involve a risk, not only from the tools themselves, but from spiky branches, loose stones thrown up by a mower, and other natural debris, which can move around unpredictably during such tasks.

strimmer

lawnmower

❀ Accidents also occur from tools – especially long-handled ones – left lying around the garden. Stepping on the head of an abandoned rake, for example, causes the handle to fly up with amazing force and speed. A tidy garden is therefore a safer garden.

❀ It is wise to wear sturdy boots when gardening, particularly when mowing. There is a wide range of gardening gloves available and you may need more than one pair – a fairly lightweight pair for light weeding, for example, and a stronger pair for pruning a large prickly, shrub.

Electrical safety

❀ You should never use electrical tools in damp weather. Ensure they are scrupulously maintained and serviced, and check leads and connections regularly to ensure they are in good repair.

❀ Fit all electrical tools with a residual current device (RCD), which cuts out the electrical circuit in the event of the power being interrupted, for example by accidentally running over a mower cable.

PREPARING TOOLS FOR WINTER STORAGE

1 *All tools should be properly serviced before winter so that they will be ready for action in the busy spring months ahead. Clean away loose debris and encrusted soil from blades, around mechanisms and on handles.*

2 *Check fixings and moving parts and tighten any parts that have worked themselves loose during the summer and autumn months.*

3 *Lubricate any parts that have ceased to move freely. Sharpen tools or have them profession-ally sharpened.*

BASIC MATERIALS

ALWAYS buy the best-quality materials you can afford. 'Doing it yourself' is an economical and satisfying way of producing the unplanted elements of a garden, but it is not necessarily quick, so value the time investment you are putting in and use materials that will be long lasting and attractive. Treat surfaces with preservatives initially and maintain them appropriately. There is no point spending time and effort creating a marvellous gazebo if you use such poor-quality untreated timber that the whole thing disintegrates in a dispiritingly short time.

Wood is an important garden DIY material, used in the construction of fences, gates, outbuildings, plant supports, decking, steps and pergolas, to name but a few applications. Always buy wood that originates from sustainable sources. Salvaged wood, such as railway sleepers, is increasingly popular and an economical and ecologically sound alternative to buying new timber.

Softwood

❀ Softwood, such as spruce or pine, is generally softer and lighter than hardwood. It is cheaper and easier to work because its texture makes it simpler to cut and nail. It is available in rough or smooth planed finishes, and in a wide variety of thicknesses and widths. Always use tanalised softwood for exterior uses. This has been pressure treated with preservative, which is a much more effective weatherproofing than simply brushing on a non-penetrating preservative.

BELOW: *The use of vivid colour can make a bold and dramatic statement in a children's play area.*

❀ Some softwoods, such as larch and western red cedar, are inherently more rot resistant than others, and are correspondingly more expensive.

Hardwood

❀ Hardwoods are cut from deciduous broad-leaved trees such as teak, mahogany or oak. Generally, hardwood is denser and harder than softwood, which makes it more difficult to cut and fix. It is also much more rot resistant and durable than softwood, so is an excellent choice for external applications – particularly those where the beauty of the wood grain is an important design feature, as in a pergola or a garden table. Iroko is a popular hardwood, as hardwearing as teak, but much cheaper, although not quite as smooth textured.

Manufactured board

❀ Manufactured boards, formed from wood chips or dust mixed with resins or glues that bond the fibres together, have become increasingly popular in recent times for their strength and value for money. Take care to use grades specifically designed for exterior use.

TREATING WOOD

SOFTWOOD is vulnerable to rot when used in the garden, particularly when it is in prolonged contact with the soil. Always buy pressure-treated timber if using softwood. If this is not possible, apply your own treatment. Choose from a weatherproof paint system or a preservative. Preservatives are available in many colours and finishes,

BELOW: *Pergolas are dramatic garden features even when unplanted, yet are relatively easy to build and install.*

including transparent and imitation hardwood colours, as well as shamelessly synthetic, but none the less attractive shades, such as blue and lavender.

Applying treatments

✤ Most treatments are simply brushed on, but new wood will benefit from immersion in an appropriate treatment for at least an hour. Makeshift treatment baths are easy to improvise, using plastic sheeting supported on piled-up bricks.

✤ Always check that the preservative you are using is not hazardous to plants if you are applying it in a situation where it will be in direct contact with plants. Take appropriate safety precautions when applying treatments that are toxic and/or flammable. Work in a well-ventilated space. This may seem like unnecessary advice since you are working in the garden, but inclement weather may force you into an enclosed garage or other outbuilding, where it is all too easy for fumes to build up to a hazardous level.

✤ Wear gloves, goggles and a face mask when dealing with noxious substances, and have a good throughput of fresh air. You should not eat or drink while using chemicals.

✤ Ecologically friendly, water-based products are available but, unfortunately, most of the products that do a really effective, long-lasting weatherproofing job are still oil or spirit based, with the attendant problems of smell and toxicity.

BELOW: *Treating wooden fences not only makes them look better, but also protects your investment against the elements.*

KNOWING THE CLIMATE

❦

The climate in your garden is of critical importance in determining what you can grow, and how well it will do. Although some plants may tolerate a climate for which they are not ideally suited, they will never really thrive in it. For example, growing a sun-loving plant in a less-than-sunny spot will produce a plant that does not flower profusely, and may become straggly as it stretches out in an attempt to find the sun. It is far better, if you have a shady garden, to plant accordingly. Climate, of course, is not just about sunlight, but a complex blend of temperature, air humidity and wind, all of which affect the gardener's choices.

General climate

❀ The general climate is literally the climate general to your area. General climate is governed by latitude, altitude, proximity to the sea and the direction of the prevailing wind. Latitude affects temperature, thus gardens in the south are warmer than those in the north. As altitude increases, so the temperature drops, and rainfall and wind speed increase at high altitudes. Proximity to the sea increases rainfall and moderates temperature.

Local climate

❀ The local climate is a term used to describe the climate within your garden. The general climate may be modified within your own garden by a number of factors. For example, if you are generally in a very windy area but your garden is surrounded by bushes and trees, the level of wind within your garden is very much reduced from that outside it.

Microclimate

❀ Microclimate describes climate modified still further within your garden – the climate specific to particular areas of your garden. Although 'understanding and manipulating the microclimate' sounds quite technical, the concept is really very basic. Plan your planting according to existing microclimatic conditions for best results. For example, train fruit trees up a sunny, south-facing wall or fence. Having

absorbed the sun's heat, a heat which is further retained by the wall and possibly added to by the heat generated from the house itself, the plant will flower and fruit well. A shade-loving plant would not flourish in this situation.

❀ As well as planting in harmony with the microclimate, it is possible to adapt and exploit it. For example, the sun may fall in one particular part of the garden only, perhaps in an awkward place and not on to the ground itself. Building a raised bed, possibly with a support behind it to further reflect and absorb the heat, will give you the opportunity to grow sun-loving flowers and food crops successfully.

BELOW: *If you live in an area of high snowfall, choose suitably sturdy plants that can withstand winter's worst.*

ABOVE: *Plants naturally accustomed to hot environments will need similarly sunny, dry conditions in order to flourish in the garden.*

Temperature and humidity

✿ Temperature and humidity are important factors in plant growth. Some plants need high temperatures and humidity in order to thrive. Dry, hot sites should be planted appropriately for best results. In very hot weather, some seeds will not germinate and plant transplantation is difficult as the soil dries out rapidly. Low temperatures bring their own problems, the most serious of which is frost.

Frost

✿ Frost is a weather condition that most gardeners quickly become aware and wary of. Late spring frosts are especially cruel to gardens. Just as the plants are starting into active growth and tender new shoots and buds are appearing, an unexpected frost can annihilate or very severely damage them. Ice crystals form within the plant cells. When the cell sap thaws, it expands. If the expansion is rapid, the cell walls split. Obviously, plants that are known to be tender (i.e. not frost resistant) will suffer most, and may be killed altogether. Half-hardy plants are of less certain frost resistance. They may or may not withstand frost conditions. To guarantee the survival of a half-hardy species in your garden, either protect it *in situ* or bring it under cover. Propagation is often undertaken to produce extra plants as an insurance policy against frost loss. Even supposedly frost-hardy plants may come under attack as their emerging, tender new top

growth appears. In very severe frosts, woody plants may split their bark.

✿ In spring, every keen gardener watches the weather closely, trying to ascertain the magical moment in the season when the risk of frost has truly passed, so that bedding and tender vegetables can be safely planted out. It is soul destroying to see your healthy young plants, whether bought from the garden centre, or lovingly raised from seed or cuttings, blackened and shrivelled, possibly killed entirely, by a single brutal late frost. The only comfort is in knowing that every gardener gets caught out like this at least once. After planting out, pay attention to the local weather forecasts and keep a close eye on the weather, particularly as night falls. If frost is predicted, protect your plants accordingly. A general piece of advice is to delay planting for at least one week after you feel that it is really safe to plant out.

✿ Frost can affect plant roots, loosening the soil and lifting plants out of the ground, where their exposed roots are vulnerable to damage from low temperatures and drying winds (wind chill). Check for frost loosening and refirm affected plants.

BELOW: *Tropical plants require moist, fertile, sunny conditions that mimic their natural habitat.*

ABOVE: *Getting to know your garden in all seasons is vital: what may be a cool shady spot in summer may be prone to frost pockets in winter.*

ABOVE: *A beautiful garden equals a well-watered one, so be prepared for some hose-work if there is a sustained dry period.*

Frost pockets

❀ Because it is heavy, cold air falls – so frost collects at the lowest point it can reach. This forms a frost pocket of air – an area particularly prone to all the risks associated with frost. Low sites, such as valleys and the land at the bottom of slopes, are potential frost pockets. If the cold air that forms in a valley cannot move freely away it will be forced back up the slope, increasing the area of potential damage. If the cold air descending a slope meets a solid barrier, such as a fence or a row of closely planted trees, it will form a frost pocket in front of it. Thinning out the trees or removing the obstacle altogether will allow the cold air to pass through. Vulnerable plants should not be grown in frost pockets unless you are prepared to protect them.

Rainfall

❀ Water is essential for plant survival. It is the main component of cell sap and is necessary for photosynthesis, the process by which plants manufacture food and transport nutrients. Seed germination and the development of shoots, roots, fruit, flowers and foliage all need a steady supply of water. Most garden plants depend largely on rainfall for their water requirements.

❀ Along with frost, drought is the other weather condition that gardeners will probably be most aware of and vigilant about in terms of plant care. A drought is a prolonged period – generally considered in the UK to be 15 consecutive days – without rain. However, plants can suffer in a much shorter time than this, particularly if they have been recently planted, so throughout the summer in particular, water your plants adequately in dry conditions. Some plants found in areas of low rainfall, such as cacti with their succulent, water-retentive tissues, are naturally adapted to drought conditions and are good choices for places where drought is a regular occurrence, or in particularly arid parts of the garden.

Wind

❀ Some wind in the garden is useful. It discourages disease, distributes pollen and seeds and reduces humidity. However, wind can also cause problems. On exposed sites, plants may be susceptible to damage such as wind scorch, which can kill new buds and blacken and wither leaves and stems. Of course, in very high winds such as in gale conditions plants can be partially broken or literally lifted out of the ground. Coastal sites are particularly prone to windy conditions and the wind from the sea is salt laden, which can further damage plants, even killing them if it reaches their roots.

❀ When planning a windbreak to ease the potential of plant damage, the temptation is to install a tall, solid barrier. However, this is counterproductive. A downdraught is caused in the lee of the barrier, resulting in increased, not reduced, turbulence. The solution is to allow approximately 50 per cent of the wind to permeate the windbreak. On a very exposed site, plan a series of windbreaks spaced approximately 10 times their height apart.

❀ Plant sympathetically. Harsh winds are very drying, so choose plants for a windy site that are well adapted to drought conditions. Plants of low-growing habit, planted closely together for more protection, will fare better on exposed sites than tall, vulnerable, willowy plants.

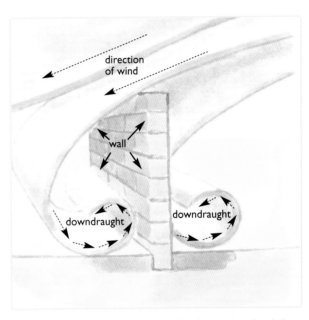

ABOVE: *A solid wall or fence creates downdraughts on either side, which can harm plants.*

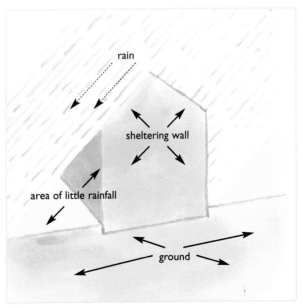

ABOVE: *Potentially damaging frost pockets can occur on either side of a solid barrier on a sloping site.*

ABOVE: *The area beside a sheltering wall receives little rain – this is the rain-shadow effect. Choose drought-tolerant plants for such a site.*

KNOWING YOUR SOIL

Spend time assessing the type of soil that prevails in your garden. Some plants will positively thrive in particular types of soil, while others grown in the same soil will merely survive. Although you can alter your soil to suit particular plants by adding different topsoils, this is not generally recommended, particularly on larger areas of garden. It is expensive and labour intensive to implement and maintain. Contemporary garden thinking leans more towards planting in harmony with pre-existing conditions rather than artificially adapting them.

Soil types

❀ The character of soil is determined by the proportions of clay, sand and silt present within it. Sandy soil is virtually clay free, and composed of large, gritty particles, which make it free draining and easy to dig. Sandy soil warms rapidly in spring, but dries out quickly in drought conditions and both water and nutrients drain away freely.

❀ Silty soil also has a low clay content, but is more moisture retaining and fertile than sandy soil. It tends to compact, which means that water can run off its surface, making it difficult to feed adequately.

❀ Clay soil retains water well and is rich in nutrients, but becomes easily compacted. A dried-out clay soil is virtually brick-like and quite impossible to work. Even when not compacted, clay soil is heavy to work and slow to warm up.

❀ Medium loam is the most desirable soil type for gardening, as it comprises approximately 50 per cent sand and 50 per cent silt and clay mix. It has a good crumb structure and holds food and water well.

Soil structure

❀ A cross-section of garden soil reveals three layers (or horizons) – topsoil, subsoil and a layer derived from the bedrock (parent rock).

❀ Generally, topsoil is dark because of its high organic content and is full of useful soil organisms.

❀ Subsoil is lighter in colour. It contains far fewer nutrients and less organic matter than topsoil and should not be brought to the surface when you are digging.

❀ If subsoil and topsoil are similarly coloured, the topsoil may be organically deficient.

❀ Some plots may have a soil pan, a hard horizontal layer on or beneath the surface of the soil, which prevents air and water moving freely to the area below.

BELOW: *Growing plants in conditions similar to their natural habitat leads to healthy specimens. These lupins are growing in well-drained, sandy soil, which mimics the conditions in which they grow wild.*

❀ This impermeable layer can be caused by a number of factors, for example, it can be the result of heavy rain on silty soil. It needs breaking up by double digging.

Soil pH

❀ The abbreviation pH stands for parts hydrogen and is used to indicate the level of acidity or alkalinity in soil – measured on a scale from 1 to 14. A reading of 7 indicates neutral soil; above 7, alkaline; below 7, acidic soil. It is important to ascertain the pH value of your soil, since pH affects the solubility of nutrients and therefore their availability to your plants.

❀ A good pH range for most plants is between 5.5 and 7.5. If your soil is dramatically acidic or alkaline, it is possible to adjust the pH, for example by adding lime to acidic soil.

❀ However, since maintenance of this adjustment is ongoing, it is more practical to select plants suited to extremes of soil pH, such as rhododendrons, which thrive on acidic soil, or fuchsias, which enjoy alkaline conditions.

TESTING FOR SOIL TEXTURE

1 *Rub a handful of soil between your fingers. A sandy soil will feel gritty and granular and is impossible to form into a ball, even when moistened slightly.*

2 *A soil that feels smoother and more solid, and easily retains a shape pushed into it, has a high proportion of clay present.*

3 *Between these extremes fall the soil types that contain various minerals in differing proportions. Sandy clay is gritty and granular yet sticky and easy to mould.*

TESTING SOIL pH LEVELS

1 *Soil pH testing kits are inexpensive and easy to use. Add water to a small amount of soil in a test tube and shake well.*

2 *As the soil settles, the water changes colour to reveal the level of acidity or alkalinity.*

3 *It is worth taking samples from various areas of the garden, as pH can vary within a single plot.*

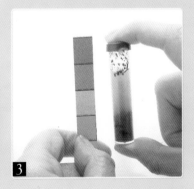

IMPROVING YOUR SOIL

❦

Having assessed your soil, you will be aware of its properties and possibly its problems. You will know its pH and its texture. Even if you are not making drastic changes, but want to improve drainage or moisture-retaining conditions, as well as create a fertile environment for plants, soil improvement is an important ongoing task.

IMPROVING SOIL STRUCTURE AND TEXTURE

DIGGING will improve soil structure, but for a significant improvement that will doubly repay the effort of digging over soil, add appropriate organic and inorganic matter at the same time.

The importance of humus

❁ Humus describes the partially decomposed organic matter that is full of micro-organisms. There are millions of bacteria and other organisms in a handful of earth, which break down leaves, dead roots and insects and transform them into nutrients, which feed living plants. Without humus, soil is essentially finely ground rock. Humus promotes good air flow through the soil and improves soil texture. It makes light soils more moisture retentive and heavy soil more workable. The humus balance is largely unchallenged in uncultivated soil, but garden planting makes demands on the humus content, which needs to be regularly redressed.

Organic soil improvers

❁ Organic options include leaf mould, well-rotted farm manure, garden compost, peat, composted shredded bark and seaweed. All improve moisture retention and soil aeration. Some contain valuable nutrients and also stimulate the bacterial activity, which makes organic material into accessible plant food.

❁ Generally, matured organic matter is used since raw humus makers can damage plants: fresh manure emits ammonia and can burn plants; fresh leaves and straw increase bacterial activity, robbing the soil of nitrogen. Raw matter is best used before planting, or in areas well away from plant roots.

RIGHT: *Well-made garden compost is a fantastic soil conditioner, adding workability and fertility to the soil.*

Compost

❁ The satisfaction of applying your own garden compost to the soil is immense. Even the smallest garden should find room for a compost bin. Ecologically and economically sound, these may be constructed from scratch or purchased ready-made. Rotating bins are ideal for the smaller garden.

❁ Compost bins should never be regarded as rubbish dumps. Aim to produce a non-smelly, crumbly brown mixture that will enrich and improve your soil texture. Do not create problems for yourself by returning perennial weeds, diseased plants or plants treated with hormone weed killer to the soil.

Leaf mould

❁ Leaf mould is best composted separately as it breaks down slowly. It is not high in nutrients and is generally acidic so is not ideal for every soil or plant type, although acid-loving plants such as camellias and rhododendrons will love it. It is a good source of humus, improves soil texture and moisture retention, and is easy to make. Collect fallen leaves in autumn, particularly oak and beech leaves since these decompose quite fast. Store in a wire mesh bin or black plastic sack punctured with air holes and the leaf mould will be ready to use the following autumn.

Inorganic soil improvers

❀ Inorganic soil additives such as grit, gravel and coarse sand are useful for improving the workability and drainage of heavy soils.

❀ Fine sand can aggravate drainage problems by blocking soil pores, so use a coarser aggregate.

❀ Lime is often used on heavy clay soil to help bind the tiny particles together to a workable crumb. It also contains nutrients and acts on humus.

❀ Apply the soil improver in carefully measured doses, according to the manufacturer's directions, and only after testing the pH of your soil to assess whether lime is needed at all.

A COMPOST HEAP

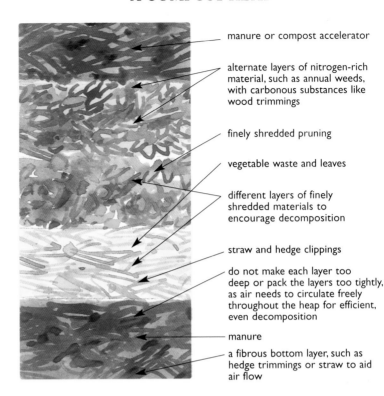

manure or compost accelerator

alternate layers of nitrogen-rich material, such as annual weeds, with carbonous substances like wood trimmings

finely shredded pruning

vegetable waste and leaves

different layers of finely shredded materials to encourage decomposition

straw and hedge clippings

do not make each layer too deep or pack the layers too tightly, as air needs to circulate freely throughout the heap for efficient, even decomposition

manure

a fibrous bottom layer, such as hedge trimmings or straw to aid air flow

MAKING A COMPOST BIN

The front of this box has removable sliding planks to give easy access to the front of the heap.

1 *You will need four 85 cm (33 in) and two 80 cm (31 in) battens, plus ten 1 m x 16 cm (39 in x 6 in) and ten 60 cm x 16 cm (24 in x 6 in) planks, plus nails or screws. The wood should be water resistant.*

2 *To create the first side panel, place five of the 1 m (39 in) planks across two of the 85 cm (33 in) battens. Ensure the sawn ends of the plank are flush with the outside edge of the battens. There*

should be a 5 cm (2 in) gap between the bottom plank and end of each batten. Using two nails or screws for each, attach the planks to the battens. Repeat to make the second side panel.

3 *To create the back panel, hold these two side panels upright, one metre (39 in) apart, by nailing scrap wood to straddle their tops. Starting at the top, nail or screw five of the 60 cm (24 in) planks onto the side panels.*

For the front panel, nail or screw the two 80 cm (31 in) battens just inside each front upright to create a housing for three of the 60 cm (24 in) sliding planks, ensuring the planks fit between the battens.

4 *To ensure stability of the structure when the front planks are removed, nail the two remaining 60 cm (24 in) planks to the top and bottom of the front panel.*

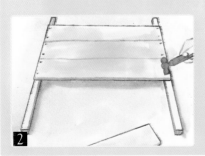

DRAINAGE

❀

Adequate drainage is of vital importance in maintaining a healthy garden. Soil that drains too readily will require strenuous efforts to keep it adequately watered and fed, while very badly drained soil can actually kill some plants – their roots starved by a lack of oxygen caused by immersion in stagnant water. Healthy bacterial activity is slowed down in these conditions, while harmful organisms multiply readily, leading to diseases such as clubroot. Even if the roots are not killed by poor drainage, they will not be able to flourish. Root growth will be restricted and the resulting shallow root system will not be able to tap into deeper water sources in the event of drought.

ASSESSING DRAINAGE

THERE are varying levels of drainage problem, many of which may be remedied without recourse to major building works. Of course, there are some plants that thrive in both extremes of drainage condition. For example, alpines enjoy very freely drained soil, while bog plants love moist, marshy conditions. Thus you could choose to leave drainage conditions unaltered and plant accordingly.

❀ There is a simple, standard test for assessing the current drainage condition of a plot. It is worth performing at the planning stages of a garden. You will need to dig a hole approximately 60 cm (24 in) deep and 60 cm (24 in) square, and leave it exposed until heavy rain has fallen.

❀ If there is no water in the hole one hour after rain, your soil is excessively drained and you will need to take steps to conserve water, such as applying mulch. If there is no water in the hole a few days after rain, you have good drainage and need take no remedial action. If some water remains at the bottom of the hole a few days after rain, drainage is poor and you will need to take action to improve it, such as double digging and applying organic top dressings.

❀ If, after a few days, the hole is still quite full, even with additional water seeping in from the surrounding soil, drainage is impeded. Also observe the colour of the soil, especially towards the base of the hole. Soil with a blue-grey or yellow tinge, possibly with rust brown marks and a stagnant smell, indicates very poor drainage.

ABOVE: *Rather than trying to retain moisture in a naturally dry site, choose plants that enjoy arid conditions for the best results with minimal effort.*

DRAINAGE PROBLEMS

Excessive drainage

❀ Adding humus (partly decomposed organic matter) to the soil will help reduce water loss, as will non-organic mulches such as pebbles. The type of humus you choose depends on what you have available and what you want to grow. For example, mushroom compost is too high in lime to use on areas planted with rhododendrons.

Poor drainage

❀ Adding organic matter generously to the soil will improve conditions where drainage is not too severely restricted. Digging in lots of coarse sand or gravel will also help. Double digging breaks up the soil, producing a more readily drained soil structure. If surface water is the problem, it may be possible to shape garden surfaces so that water can run away freely into simple ditches or drains. You could also consider introducing raised beds, or adding more soil to heighten the soil level generally, to keep roots drier.

Impeded drainage

❀ Drainage will be severely restricted if your garden has non-porous rock close to the surface, a very high water table (the level at which water is held naturally within the ground) or a soil pan (hard layer below the surface). Artificial drainage methods then become necessary. There are several possibilities; the

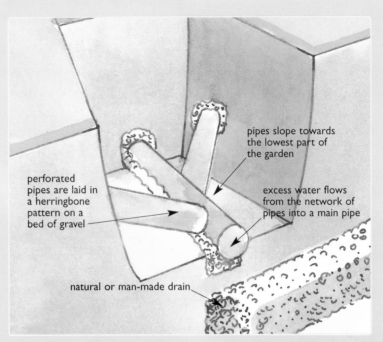

perforated pipes are laid in a herringbone pattern on a bed of gravel

pipes slope towards the lowest part of the garden

excess water flows from the network of pipes into a main pipe

natural or man-made drain

ABOVE: *If surface water is a serious problem in your garden and the water table is close to the surface, you may need to install a submerged drainage system.*

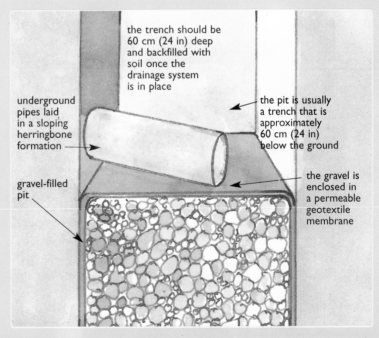

underground pipes laid in a sloping herringbone formation

the trench should be 60 cm (24 in) deep and backfilled with soil once the drainage system is in place

the pit is usually a trench that is approximately 60 cm (24 in) below the ground

gravel-filled pit

the gravel is enclosed in a permeable geotextile membrane

ABOVE: *A French drain is an unobtrusive solution to the problem of a badly waterlogged site.*

simplest is a French drain, a gravel-filled trench. More elaborate piped systems are generally best installed by professionals. If a piped system is planned on a flat site, the pipes will need to slope to allow water to flow away easily.

WATERING

All plants need water and the various watering requirements of different plants need to be considered when planning a garden. For example, if you live in an area of low rainfall or are gardening on a roof terrace exposed to drying wind, it is wise to consider planting to suit these conditions. Some plants cope well with dry conditions, for example succulents, which store water in their tissues, and silver-leaved plants, which are covered with fine hairs to help reduce evaporation.

Existing conditions

❀ Planting sympathetically to dry conditions significantly improves your chances of growing healthy plants, without necessitating an undue investment of time and effort in watering systems.

❀ Although it is possible to develop irrigation systems to deal with whatever conditions you face, it is more sensible to work on conserving the moisture available – for

BELOW: *A sprinkler is invaluable for watering wide areas such as lawns and herbaceous borders evenly and gently.*

example, surface mulching, adding moisture-conserving organic matter to your soil, and planting according to the level of moisture prevalent in your garden.

Effective watering

❀ Watering is a critical gardening task, so an accessible water supply is vital. Although an accessible kitchen tap and watering can will answer the needs of a very small plot, a garden tap is invaluable, along with a hose of sufficient length to reach the furthest part of the garden. Make sure that the tap and any exposed pipework is protected from frost in winter.

❀ Most novice gardeners water little and often, but this actually encourages shallow root growth and germination of weeds. Even a small garden will require a significant amount of watering in dry weather and a hose makes light work of this task. As a guide, an adequate level of watering in midsummer, on a fast-draining soil, would be approximately 10–20 litres per sq m (2–4 gallons per sq yd) – roughly two watering cans full. This demonstrates that simply sprinkling over the border with a single watering can full is inadequate, and will lead to plant problems. Never water in full sun as you risk leaf scorch, and the water will evaporate very quickly from the soil's surface.

Watering container plants

❀ Plants in containers lose water rapidly through evaporation. Group containers together to help conserve moisture. Make plans for watering if you are going away in summer or, at the very least, move containers to a shady place; otherwise you may arrive home to a collection of dead plants.

❀ Incorporating water-retaining granules into the compost at planting time is useful. These granules swell to form a gel capable of holding large quantities of water, which is gradually released into the compost. This is particularly useful for containers especially prone to rapid moisture loss, such as hanging baskets with their large exposed surface area yet small amount of soil, and terracotta pots, whose porosity allows for quick evaporation. Applying a surface mulch will also help retain moisture.

Automated systems

❀ If you garden on a particularly dry site and wish to grow thirsty plants, such as vegetables, or if you wish to simplify your watering duties, consider installing a permanent watering system.

❀ Drip-feed systems comprise tubes fitted with drip heads to trickle water on to particular areas, such as shrubs in a border or growing bags. Unless fitted with a timer, drip-feed systems can waste water, and they need regular cleaning to keep the tubes and heads clear.

❀ Seep hoses are another option. These are flattened hoses punctured finely along their length. They are useful for watering large areas such as lawns, and are ideal for watering rows of vegetables evenly.

ABOVE: *A watering can is a perennial gardening essential, and it is worth investing in a good quality metal one for long-term use.*

PLANTING A CONTAINER USING WATER-RETAINING GEL

1 *With the addition of a liner and drainage holes, an old basket can be used as a container for plants. To reduce the need for watering, mix water-retaining gel with the compost before you begin, following the manufacturer's directions regarding quantities. Place a layer of drainage pebbles over the base of the container, followed by a layer of compost.*

2 *Add the shrubs and larger bulbs of your choice to the basket.*

3 *Backfill with compost before adding smaller bulbs. Firm the compost gently and water.*

4 *For instant colour, fill the basket with some flowering plants.*

PLANT FOODS

Plants need a balanced diet of nutrients in order to thrive. Plants use the essential elements in soil more quickly than they can be replenished naturally, for example by the gradual decomposition of fallen leaves. Substantial amounts of potassium, phosphorus and nitrogen are lost when ground is cultivated. These major nutrients are needed in large quantities to maintain good growth, so additional feeding is required. Potassium promotes disease resistance and produces healthy fruits and flowers. Phosphorus is needed for good root development, and nitrogen for healthy growth and foliage. The amount of nutrients required depends on the plants grown and how intensively the soil is used. For example, an alpine rock garden is much less hungry than a densely sown vegetable border.

Organic fertilisers

❀ Organic fertilisers are matter derived from living organisms, be they animal or plant in origin, such as fish meal, bone meal or dried blood. They are natural products, generally slow acting, and not as likely to scorch foliage as inorganic fertilisers might if inappropriately used. Organic fertilisers generally provide plants with a steady supply of food over a long period.

growmore

natural manure

Inorganic fertilisers

❀ Inorganic fertilisers are not necessarily unnatural. Some are derived from earth minerals, such as Chilean potash nitrate; others are synthetically manufactured. Inorganic fertilisers are very concentrated and fast acting. Overdosing can result in scorched plants, so great care must be taken to follow manufacturer's directions accurately when applying. Inorganic fertilisers are often used to give plants a quick boost of nutrients.

Soil conditioners

❀ Fertiliser feeds the soil, but does not alter the soil structure. For example, it cannot make a heavy soil more open. Soil conditioners such as animal manure add nutrients, but the amount of food is minute in comparison to the quantity of material which will need to be applied. The benefit of adding manure and compost to the soil is that in addition to their soil nutritional qualities, they can improve moisture retention and soil workability. In the longer term, they decompose to form humus, the dead and live bacteria within soil which is its life force, facilitating the effective absorption of plant foods, promoting air flow and improving drainage.

bone meal

TYPES OF FERTILISER

Fertilisers are available in different forms, including liquids, powders and pellets. The form chosen will depend on the type of plant, the season of application and the soil type.

Dry fertilisers

❀ These are nutrients in a dried form – granules, pellets or powder – which are sprinkled directly on to the soil. They are very concentrated and it is critically important to apply them evenly and in appropriate quantities, following the manufacturer's directions, to avoid plant damage.

Liquid fertilisers

❀ These may be bought either in liquid form, or as powder which is to be diluted in water before application. They are generally safer and easier to use than dry fertilisers, and are usually quick acting. Some liquid fertilisers are designed for foliar feeding. Application to the leaves means that the nutrients enter the sap stream quickly, which can be a useful technique if you are trying to resuscitate a sick plant.

Feeding container plants

❀ Container-grown plants need particular feeding care. The amount of soil in a container is limited, so any available nutrients are quickly exhausted by the plant. Regular watering also washes away nutrients through the drainage holes. Slow-release fertilisers worked into the compost when planting, or added as top dressing, are a good solution. If additional feeding is needed, for example if the plant shows visible signs of deficiency, this longer-term feeding programme may be supplemented by foliar feeding or by adding a quick-release fertiliser. Fertiliser spikes, small sticks that gradually release nutrients into the soil, are a convenient way of feeding container plants.

ABOVE: *Organic fertilisers include compost made from coconut husks, which can be used for potting and seeding.*

food released into soil in dilute form

water penetrates pores

polymer coat

ABOVE: *The food-releasing pattern of slow-release fertiliser is hard to assess as it is affected by the soil's moisture content, pH level and temperature. However, it is an undeniably simple way of feeding plants and is becoming increasingly popular.*

ABOVE: *There are many general-purpose fertilisers on the market; these are suitable for most conditions and uses.*

DIGGING

❦

Digging may not be the easiest or most exciting garden task, but it has many important functions, particularly on soil that is being newly cultivated. Digging improves the texture and workability in two ways. The spade physically breaks up compacted soil initially. Frost and drying winds further break up the exposed clods. Digging also offers an opportunity for incorporating substances into the soil that can help its fertility, humus-making ability, drainage and moisture retention. What you add will depend on the type of soil you have. Digging also makes it easy to remove perennial weeds and bury annual ones.

HOW TO DIG

IT IS all too easy to injure your back when digging. Digging is hard physical exercise and needs to be taken as seriously as any physical workout. Digging is usually done in autumn, when the weather has become colder; yet each year, thousands of gardeners embark on a bout of heavy digging without warming up their muscles gradually. Combine this sudden shock to the chilled body with a careless digging technique and you have a recipe for severe back pain.

✿ Wrap up warmly for digging. Acclimatise your body to exertion gradually by embarking on some more gentle gardening tasks before starting to dig. Do not overestimate the amount you will be able to dig, especially on your first session. You could all too easily hurt your back so badly that you will not be able to complete the task at all. Finally, and crucially, take care to use the correct posture when digging, treat your body with respect and never lift more weight than you can comfortably handle.

USING A SPADE CORRECTLY

1 *Press one foot down evenly on the blade and insert the spade vertically into the soil. The handle of the spade will be sloping slightly away from you if the blade has been inserted at a true vertical, giving you valuable additional leverage.*

2 *Pull the handle towards you. Slide one hand down the spade towards the blade. Holding the spade on the ferrule with this hand, and*

with the other hand still at the top of the spade, bend your knees and evenly lever out the soil. Work smoothly, not with jerky, sudden movements, which can jar your back.

3 *Gradually lift the soil on to the spade, taking the strain by gently straightening your legs, not jerking your back up suddenly. Never lift more soil than you are comfortable with at one time.*

DIGGING TECHNIQUES

AUTUMN and early winter are the best seasons for digging. At this time of year the soil is generally in an ideal condition – neither baked hard dry by the sun, nor saturated with water. The turned clods will also gradually be broken down by the elements over winter, to improve soil texture. Never dig when the ground is frozen or waterlogged as this will severely damage the structure of the soil, and always use the correct tool for the job. Your spade should be comfortably sized, so that it is not an effort to lift it, and an appropriate length for your height, to reduce the risk of back strain.

Although digging has many significant benefits, its role has gradually been viewed as being of diminished importance in recent times. For many years, garden experts prescribed complex and labour-intensive digging methods such as trenching (digging three spits deep). Simple, single and double digging are the techniques widely used and recommended today. Contemporary thinking generally veers towards double digging newly cultivated soil only once. Keen vegetable gardeners may repeat this double digging every few years, but most gardeners will use the single digging technique in subsequent years.

Simple digging

❀ Simple digging is the easiest and quickest digging technique. Since it does not involve any trench work, it is the only really practical way of digging in the sort of confined space created in a garden border filled with many permanent plantings.

❀ Simple digging literally involves simply digging. A spadeful of soil is picked up and turned over back on to its original position, then briskly chopped up with the spade.

❀ When you have dug the soil, leave it alone for approximately three weeks before growing anything in it. This will allow newly buried annual weeds to die, and give the soil time to settle. The weather will act on the soil surface to break it down into smaller clods. The soil will then be much easier to cultivate to the fine tilth needed for planting or sowing.

ABOVE: As you lift the soil from the trench, slide your hand towards the blade and straighten up slowly without jerking your back.

Single digging

❀ Single digging is a methodical way of ensuring that an area is cultivated evenly and to a specific depth. The ground is dug to a single spade's depth as you work systematically to produce rows of trenches. As each trench is dug, the soil being lifted is placed in the neighbouring trench.

❀ Although a spade is generally used, a fork may be a more comfortable choice when working on heavy soil.

RIGHT: *Digging over the soil before planting improves soil structure and allows you to incorporate the humus-making substances, such as manure, which are so beneficial to plants.*

SINGLE DIGGING

1 *Starting at a marked line, drive the spade vertically into the soil to the full depth of the blade. Remove the soil and place in a wheelbarrow, ready to carry to the opposite end of the plot.*

2 *Dig along the line to produce a trench 30 cm (12 in) wide, and the depth of the spade.*

3 *Dig a second trench parallel with the first. Fill the first trench with the soil from the second trench, incorporating organic matter as required. Twist the spade to aerate the soil as you place it in the first trench.*

4 *Continue digging trenches until you reach the other end of the plot, filling the final trench with the soil from the first trench.*

Double digging

❀ This deep form of digging improves drainage by breaking up any hard subsurface pan in the soil. Double digging is generally regarded as necessary for previously uncultivated soil prior to sowing or planting, and wherever drainage is poor. In double digging the soil is literally dug to double the depth of the spade or fork, and the trenches are twice as wide as those produced for single digging.

❀ It is critically important not to bring subsoil to the surface, as this will adversely affect soil fertility. You will need to ascertain the depth of the topsoil before starting to double dig. If the topsoil is more than two spade depths (known as 'spits') deep, then you have no problem. You can simply transfer the soil from one trench to the other as for single digging.

❀ If the topsoil is only one spit deep, you will need to ensure that the topsoil and subsoil are kept separate and distinct so that the subsoil goes back on the bottom of the neighbouring trench, with the topsoil on top – not mixed together or the other way around.

❀ You will need both a spade and a fork for double digging. Always dig at the right season for your soil. Dig medium and heavy soils in autumn and early winter; dig over very heavy soil before winter sets in.

❀ Sandy soil may be dug in winter or early spring. If you dig too early you may encourage a fine crop of weeds. Always make sure that the soil is not saturated with water, nor frozen solid, before planning to dig. Similarly, it is not prudent to dig when the soil has dried hard after a prolonged period without rain.

DOUBLE DIGGING

1 *Mark out the plot with a garden line. Dig the first trench about 60 cm (24 in) wide, and as deep as the head of the spade. As with single digging, collect the soil from this trench in a barrow, ready to take to the opposite end of the plot when the barrow is full.*

2 *Standing in the trench, break up the soil at the bottom of the trench to the depth of the fork tines. Incorporate organic matter such as manure if required.*

3 *Mark out another trench parallel to the first. Dig out this trench, placing the soil from here in the first trench.*

4 *Fork the bottom of the new trench and continue to the next trench. Work your way across the plot until you reach the opposite end. Fill the final trench with soil removed from the first trench.*

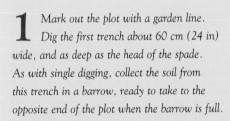

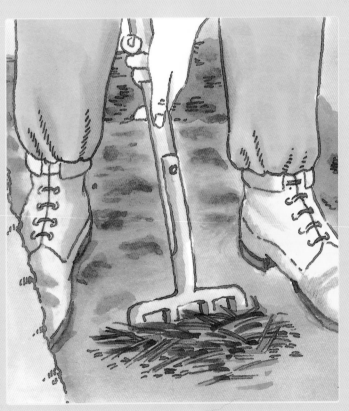

TOP DRESSINGS AND MULCHES

Top dressing describes the superficial application of fertiliser and other additives, such as sand, to the surface of the soil or lawn. It is also used as a general term, encompassing any sort of superficial dressing of the soil, including mulching. Top dressings and mulches are applied to the surface of the soil for several reasons. They all help plant growth in one or more ways. All help reduce moisture loss by evaporation. Some add nutrients to the soil, enrich the humus content of the soil and improve soil texture and workability. Some, such as gravel, have no nutritional value but are used to aid drainage, regulate soil temperature, deter pests such as slugs, and suppress the growth of weeds, moss, lichen and other undesirable organisms on the surface of the soil. In addition, a simple gravel top dressing is also very decorative in its own right.

USING TOP DRESSINGS AND MULCHES

Top dressings and mulches may be the unsung heroes of the garden border. They don't look terribly exciting in the garden centre, but they have an immense amount to offer every gardener – from the apartment dweller with a solitary window box dressed with an attractive, moisture-retaining, weed- and pest-deterring aggregate, to someone with a large vegetable garden using plastic sheeting for purely practical reasons.

ABOVE: *A natural mulch, such as shredded cedar bark, helps suppress weed growth and conserve moisture, yet is an attractive, unobtrusive material.*

Applying mulch

❀ Always apply mulch to warm, moist soil. If mulch is applied to a frozen or dry soil, you will find that it just works against you, simply sealing in the problems. Similarly, if organic mulch is applied to a soil rife with weeds, the weeds will benefit as much as the desirable plants, reaping the benefits of an enriched soil and improved moisture retention, and growing even more profusely than in an unmulched soil. The overall guiding principle of applying mulch, therefore, is to think carefully before using it, taking care not to seal in any problems, which will be aggravated by the insulating properties of all mulch.

❀ Apply a generous layer of mulch, approximately 7.5 cm (3 in) deep, spreading it out from the plant to cover roughly the same area as the potential growth spread of the plant itself. Apply up to, but not touching plant stems, as this can encourage rotting.

woodchip mulch

ORGANIC MULCHES

Mulches can be divided into organic and inorganic types. They share many attributes, some organic mulches having the added benefits of nutritional value. This is not always desirable, however, as described above. For example, garden compost has many good properties, but it also provides a perfect environment for germinating weeds. It is therefore not the best choice for weed suppression.

Bark

❀ Available in a variety of scales, from finely shredded to large chunks, bark is a popular mulch. It improves surface drainage and suppresses weeds. Coarsely shredded bark takes a long time to break down, repaying the initial investment, as it should last two years before it needs replacing.

❀ Bark is also sufficiently heavy not to blow about the garden. It is very attractive, and is often used to top dress borders. Bark is slightly acidic, a quality that diminishes when it begins to decompose, so only apply composted (matured) bark as a mulch. Soil dressed with bark will need supplementing with a nitrogenous fertiliser.

leaf mould mulch

dried bark mulch

Cocoa shells

✿ Cocoa shells smell wonderful, as if applying a blanket of grated chocolate to the soil. Apart from this sybaritic benefit, a cocoa shell mulch is very attractive, making it the next most popular ornamental border mulch after bark. Cocoa shell's are slightly acidic, so soil dressed with them will need to be supplemented with fertiliser. Until cocoa shells settle, they are also very lightweight and susceptible to being distributed around the garden by wind and birds. They are also quite expensive.

cocoa shells

Farmyard manure

✿ Once popular, farmyard manure has lost popularity as a mulch in the flower border. It does help the humus content of the soil and has some nutritional benefit, as well as its moisture-retaining and soil-texturising properties. However, it is not attractive, is often smelly, and its fertility promotes weed growth. It must be used only when well rotted, or it may damage your plants.

farmyard manure

woven black plastic

ABOVE: *Mulching helps keep weeds at bay while young plants are becoming established.*

INORGANIC MULCHES

INORGANIC mulches, especially sheet types, are excellent at retaining soil moisture. They are also superb at suppressing weeds because light is excluded totally from the soil, preventing weed germination. Obviously, they do not assist humus production or add nutrients to the soil. If you do need to enrich the soil beneath sheet mulch, pierce it and apply soluble fertiliser through the holes.

Woven black plastic

✿ Excellent for mulching between rows of vegetables, this is initially expensive but it is reusable.

Fibre fleece

✿ Used mainly to raise soil temperature, this is often used as a 'floating' mulch and pest barrier. It is used almost like a cloche – applied over, not around, crops.

fibre fleece

Black plastic

✿ This cheap mulch raises soil temperature and suppresses weeds, but is not attractive unless covered with a more decorative substance such as gravel. It is popular in vegetable plots.

Grit

❀ Grit is useful for improving drainage and is very attractive. To keep weeds at bay, grit is best applied over plastic sheeting. Coarse grit is often used as a slug and snail deterrent, since these creatures dislike moving across its sharp surface.

grit

Pebbles/gravel

❀ This is an attractive and popular inorganic choice. Choose well-washed products, free of soil particles that might bind the stones together, hosting weeds.

gravel

pebbles

TOP DRESSINGS

SOME materials are used on the soil around plants, or on lawns, not for their mulching properties, but to improve the soil nutritionally and texturally. Always follow the manufacturer's directions precisely when applying top dressings. Keep solid dressings off foliage and plant stems, since fertiliser can scorch.

Lime

❀ Lime is available in many forms, such as chalk, ground limestone and magnesium limestone. The most popular form is hydrated (slaked) lime. Lime is a plant food, and makes other plant foods available by acting on humus to free the elements necessary for good plant growth. Lime removes sourness from the soil by neutralising acidity. Few plants thrive in very acidic conditions. Lime also breaks up heavy soil and encourages beneficial bacteria and organisms such as earthworms to flourish. A pH test will determine whether or not you need to lime your soil. Even a neutral soil will benefit from reliming every few years, since rain washes lime from the soil. Alkaline soil must not be limed, as it already has sufficient lime. Lime is generally applied after digging, in the autumn.

Fertiliser

❀ Fertilisers contain one or more nutrients in a concentrated form, and are added to the soil to feed plants. They must not be confused with humus makers, since they do not share their important attributes. Fertilisers should not be used in isolation. Without humus makers, the plants cannot utilise the food provided by the fertilisers. Fertiliser as a top dressing is usually applied in the spring.

Humus makers

❀ Bulky organic matter is used as a top dressing to improve soil texture and build up the bacterial population,thereby releasing nutrients to the plants. Humus makers do not have a significant amount of nutritional value compared with their bulk, and so need to be used in conjunction with fertilisers for optimum benefits. Organic top dressings are usually applied in the autumn.

CARING FOR YOUR PLANTS

Plants are living things, and like all living things they need plenty of your loving care and attention if they are to thrive.

One of the most rewarding garden tasks is propagating – to increase your stock by dividing existing plants or by growing new plants from seed is very satisfying. Propagating is not difficult – this chapter shows you how to get the best results by selecting the right method for each type of plant.

Good housekeeping is as essential in the garden as it is in the home. Keeping the plants neat and tidy, and pruning when necessary encourages healthy growth and prolific flowering. There is great pleasure to be found in a garden that looks well-tended in every season.

PROPAGATING YOUR PLANTS

Growing your own plants from seed or increasing your stocks from existing plants is undoubtedly one of the most satisfying areas of gardening. It is not only an economical way of filling the garden, but the thrill of stocking your garden with plants that you have produced yourself is incomparable. You can regenerate old, tired-looking plants, and also produce back-up stocks of plants that may be vulnerable to frost damage or disease. Propagation is also a very sociable occupation, since you will often find that you produce many more new plants than you have room for, and so gardening friendships develop as cuttings and seedlings are exchanged.

THE BASICS

THE word propagation somehow conjures up quite off-putting connotations of science laboratories, specialist equipment and in-depth botanical knowledge. However, it simply means 'to breed, to multiply', and applies to every method of increasing plant stocks – from broadcast sowing of annual seeds directly into the soil, to taking and rooting cuttings.

❀ Specialist equipment such as greenhouses and mist benches are useful but by no means essential to many forms of propagation. A bright (but not sunny windowsill), a cold frame and, if possible, a small heated propagator will enable you to grow a very wide range of plants.

ABOVE: *Always use perfectly clean pots and trays for healthy, disease-free propagation and cover them with mesh-wire or netting if there is a danger of something falling on the delicate new plants.*

PROPAGATION EQUIPMENT

THE very simplest form of propagation – sowing seed directly into the soil – needs no special equipment, as every child who has ever grown an abundance of nasturtiums from an inexpertly cast handful of seeds will testify.

❀ However, many gardeners, thrilled by early triumphs from sowing direct into the soil, quickly become more adventurous, and keen to extend the range of plants grown. Just a few simple pieces of equipment will dramatically increase your chances of consistent success.

ABOVE: *Seed can be sown directly into the soil, but the success rate may not be as great as if the plants had been transplanted from pots.*

Pots and trays

❀ There is a wide range of pots and trays available, and the choice can seem quite overwhelming. Since hygiene is a critical concern when propagating, it may be advisable to start your propagating experience with new, single-use modular seed trays, since these will not hold any old, potentially lethal bacteria or fungi.

❀ These trays consist of individual plastic cells, which make it easy to sow seeds singly and avoid any damage when thinning out the seedlings. The trays are flimsy and are held securely in a more rigid tray. This type of tray is generally intended only for a single season's use.

❀ More lasting and expensive trays are available in rigid plastics. These will need to be thoroughly disinfected after each use, and stored out of the sunlight. Novice propagators with limited space and time will probably prefer the inexpensive, labour- and storage-space saving flexible tray option. These trays are usually sold with a useful clear plastic lid, which assists in providing the warm, humid environment necessary for successful germination.

❀ Larger pots are useful for sowing larger seeds, such as climbers or shrubs and, of course, are also needed for potting on all plants. Fibre-based pots are especially good for plants that resent root disturbance. The young plant is simply planted out still in its pot, which will

water vapour falls onto plant

ABOVE: *A rigid-topped propagator offers an excellent start to young plants. Water vapour condenses on the inside of the lid and falls onto the plants, so the general atmosphere within the unit is moist. This combination helps the plants to replace the water lost through their leaves.*

eventually break down into the soil. Home-made biodegradable pots can also be made from simple cones of newspaper.

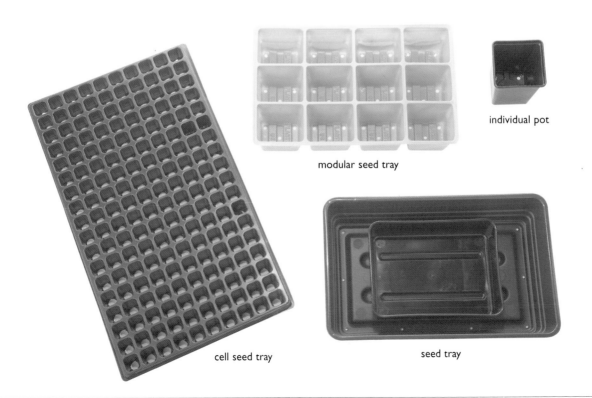

modular seed tray

individual pot

cell seed tray

seed tray

HOME-MADE PROPAGATION EQUIPMENT

POLYTHENE bags, simply suspended above pots or trays with canes or with wire twisted into hoops, are a popular and inexpensive way of providing a warm, humid atmosphere that will encourage rapid germination and healthy growth.

❀ Cut-off clear plastic bottles, upended over pots, are another effective, low-cost idea. It is important in each case to keep the leaves of the young plants away from the plastic itself, as they will rot if they come into direct contact with the moisture that collects there.

Heated propagators

❀ A little heat from underneath assists germination generally, and is essential for the germination of some plants. Small, self-contained domestic heated propagators are available, which sit on the windowsill. These are an ideal next step up from the plastic bag propagation technique. Heated bases that fit under seed trays are also available.

ABOVE: Cold frames provide an excellent introduction to growing under glass. They can easily overheat in summer because of their diminutive size. Propping the lid of the frame open in hot weather allows the rising warm air to escape, as well as keeping the plants inside well ventilated and at a reasonable temperature.

❀ Many gardeners, encouraged by early successes with propagation, quickly run out of windowsills, and spill over into the greenhouse. If propagating in a greenhouse early in the year when temperatures are still low, you will need to invest in a more sophisticated propagator with a thermostat and a powerful heating element. You will probably also need larger units than the domestic models, which house only two or three seed trays.

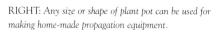

RIGHT: Any size or shape of plant pot can be used for making home-made propagation equipment.

LEFT: *Growing cuttings under plastic is an inexpensive way to increase your plant stocks.*

Mist propagators

❀ Enthusiastic propagating gardeners will enjoy the great benefits that mist propagators can bring. These incorporate all that plants are going to need for their best possible chance of successful, easy germination and early, healthy growth.

❀ The simplest mist propagators to use are the self-contained enclosed units that include a heating element, thermostat, transparent lid and a misting head.

❀ A constant film of water is maintained on the plant material and, when the misting head operates, the risk of fungal disease is reduced, as spores are effectively washed out of the air and from foliage before they can infect plant tissue. This is a more sophisticated version of what happens in the plastic bag propagator – just on a larger, more convenient scale and with the added benefit of consistent heat from underneath and controlled humidity. The misting head is activated automatically when the plants become too dry. Open misting units are also available.

Cold frame

❀ A cold frame is extremely useful for hardening off plants. The air and soil temperatures in cold frames are warmer than in open soil, making it possible to acclimatise plants gradually to the conditions outdoors after their cosseted start in the home or greenhouse.

❀ The lid should be removed on warmer days to air the plants, and covered at night with additional insulation if extremely cold weather is expected. If transparent insulation, such as plastic bubble wrap or layers of clear plastic, is used there is no need to remove this during the day, as it still transmits light to the plants.

Soil-warming cables

❀ These are designed to warm the compost in unheated propagators, or to heat the soil and air in a cold frame or a mist bench in a greenhouse. They are fitted in an S-shape pattern, with the cable not touching at any point, buried approximately 7.5 cm (3 in) below the surface of moist sand.

❀ The cables are sold with instructions as to what size area they are capable of warming effectively, and it is obviously important to follow strictly all directions concerning their installation and use.

❀ The best cables have a wired-in thermostat. All should be used in conjunction with a residual current device (RCD) in case they are accidentally cut through during cultivation. Most novice propagators will find self-contained propagation units more convenient to install and use than cable systems.

BELOW: *A cold frame propped open to increase ventilation.*

warm air circulates within the cold frame

SOWING INDOORS

FINE and medium seeds may be sown by the method shown here. Large or pelleted seeds (seeds specially prepared in a coating to make a pellet for easier sowing) should be sown individually in compartments, degradable containers, or evenly spaced in pans (shallow pots).

❀ Mixing very fine seeds with an equal quantity of fine sand before sowing makes even distribution much easier. Always check the individual germination requirements of your seeds. Some germinate in darkness, others in light. The directions given here are necessarily generalised but apply to most fine seeds, such as many half-hardy annuals, which are popular plants to grow indoors from seed.

PROPAGATION COMPOST

Plants have a much better chance of germination if sown into the correct sort of compost. Fine seeds, in particular, need to be in good overall contact with the soil.

❀ Purpose-made seed compost is finely textured to meet this requirement. It is also moisture retentive and low in nutrients, since salts can damage seedlings. As the seedlings grow, they will need to be transplanted to a soil that can feed them adequately.

Seed compost

❀ A general-purpose seed compost consists of two parts sterilised loam, one part peat or peat substitute and one part sand, plus a small amount of lime. It is advisable to buy a pre-mixed seed compost, as you can then be sure that the proportions are accurate.

Cuttings compost

❀ Cuttings composts are free draining, as they are designed for use in high-humidity environments. A general-purpose cuttings compost comprises roughly one part peat or peat substitute and one part sand (or other free-draining substance such as perlite), plus a small percentage of lime, dried blood, calcium carbonate, potassium nitrate and potassium sulphate.

❀ As with seed compost, buying a pre-mixed cuttings compost will ensure you have the correct proportions of each component.

RIGHT: Overcrowding and a lack of ventilation can cause 'damping off', a catastrophic scourge, wreaking havoc on plants by damaging and distorting new leaves and shoots, as well as weakening the plant as a whole.

HYGIENE

Hygiene is critically important in propagation. The moist, humid conditions within a propagator are as perfect for the development of fungal diseases as they are for developing healthy plants.

❀ It is therefore essential to use sterilised containers, compost and tools to reduce this risk. Fungicidal solutions are available, which may be applied to protect seedlings further. Ensure that you follow the manufacturer's directions strictly.

❀ Taking cuttings inevitably exposes bare plant tissue, which is an increased risk of infection. Good hygiene practices will decrease the risk. Clean tools with a methylated spirit solution between cuttings to avoid cross contamination, and keep benches spotlessly clean.

Preventing damping off

❀ Overcrowding causes an overly moist, stagnant atmosphere in which fungi can flourish. These air- or soil-borne fungi can cause the condition known as 'damping-off', whereby roots become diseased, darken and then die. The seedling collapses, and a fluffy growth may be seen on the compost as well as on the seedlings.

❀ There is no cure for damping off, so attention to cleanliness, pricking out seedlings to avoid overcrowding (see below), not overwatering and providing adequate air flow above and around the plants are essential requisites. Keep the surface of the compost clear of any fallen leaves or other debris, which could foster disease.

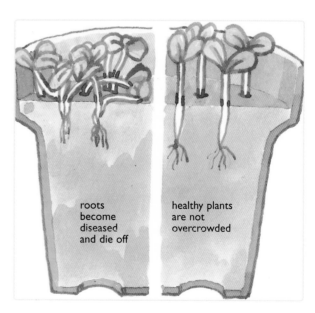

roots become diseased and die off

healthy plants are not overcrowded

SOWING SEEDS IN A TRAY

1 *Fill a seed tray with good-quality seed compost and firm it to within 1.5 cm (³/₄ in) of the top, using a presser board. Water the compost and leave to stand for approximately 30 minutes.*

2 *Scatter the seed or the seed and sand mixture evenly across the surface.*

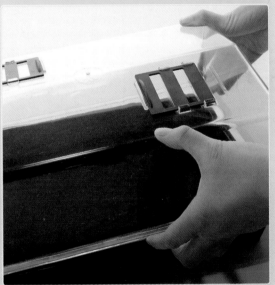

3 *Sieve over a layer of moist compost to produce a covering approximately the same depth as the size of the seeds that you have planted.*

4 *Cover the tray with glass or clear plastic, not allowing it to touch the seeds, and place the tray somewhere warm and bright. If the tray is placed in direct sunlight, shade it with fine netting.*

CARE OF PROPAGATED PLANTS

As well as taking good care of hygiene when preparing compost, containers and cuttings or seeds for propagation, care must be taken of the young plants as they germinate and grow.

Firming in

❀ It is essential that seeds are in good contact with the compost since water is drawn up by capillary action. If air pockets form around the seeds water cannot be transmitted to where it is needed, so it is important to firm the compost gently when planting seed. However, do not compress the soil heavily.

Watering

❀ Propagated plants need a consistently moist, but not wet, environment. An overly saturated compost will reduce the oxygen available to the plants and potentially encourage disease.

Caring for new seedlings

❀ Seedlings must have sufficient room around them to breathe. As soon as shoots appear, remove the propagator lid. Protect the seedlings from draughts and harsh sunlight, but keep them in bright light. Continue to water, ensuring that the roots do not dry out.

ABOVE: *Ensure that your new plants have enough water, but make sure that they are not over-watered, as this may encourage disease.*

Pricking out

❀ When seedlings appear, the plants are still very vulnerable. As well as the risk of damping off, overcrowded seedlings will be competing for light and nutrients. If they do not succumb to disease, they will probably become underfed, weak, spindly plants that will never achieve their full, healthy potential. They therefore need to be thinned out. This planting-on process is known as pricking out.

❀ The initial leaves you see after germination are seed leaves, or cotyledons, which swell on germination, forcing the seed coat open. These provide the initial food reserves for the plant. The next pair of leaves to appear will be the first 'true' leaves, and seedlings may be pricked out when the true leaves are well developed. Discard weak, unhealthy-looking seedlings.

❀ Fill the next appropriate size up of container with good-quality potting compost – a 7.5 cm (3 in) diameter pot or planting compartment will suit a single seedling, while a larger pot may hold three growing plants comfortably.

❀ Knock the container of seedlings gently to loosen the compost. Carefully separate the seedlings, handling them only by the seed leaves to avoid damaging the seedlings. Carefully lift each healthy seedling from the soil, trying to maintain a little compost around its roots if possible. Plant them at the same depth in the soil as they were in the first tray and gently firm the compost around them. Tap the container to settle the compost, and water the seedlings to settle the compost around their roots.

❀ To give the plants a good chance of recovery from the pricking-out process, increase the humidity as for germinating, by covering the container with clear plastic, just for a few days. Ensure that the plastic does not touch the leaves.

Hardening off

❀ Gradually acclimatising plants to the very different conditions outside the protected environment of the propagator is vital and should be taken every bit as seriously as the initial, exciting part of the propagation procedure.

❀ Hardening off takes time. The natural waxes coating the leaves of the young plants need to adapt their form and thickness in order to reduce water loss – a process that takes place over several days and cannot be hurried. The pores on the leaves, which control water loss and through which oxygen and carbon dioxide pass in and out of the leaves, also need time to adapt to the harsher conditions outside.

❀ As a rule, hardening off takes about two weeks. When the young plants have become well established inside, they can be moved to an unheated cold frame, where they are still protected by polythene or glass. Gradually increase the amount of ventilation by opening or removing the cover for increasingly long periods until the plants are fully acclimatised. Close the frame at night to begin with, graduating to leaving it open at

night, except when frost is anticipated. Insulate the cold frame if the weather is very harsh.

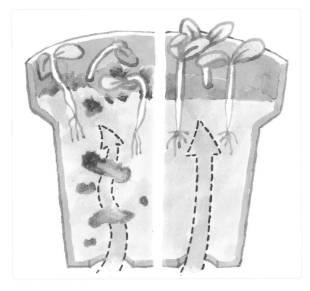

ABOVE: *It is important to press down compost evenly before planting seeds, so that water can be drawn up towards the roots of the seedlings by capillary action. Air pockets in the soil will break this action and the seedlings will therefore not flourish as they should.*

PRICKING OUT

All young seedlings are vulnerable so handle them with care as you are replanting them.

1 *Make a hole in the soil with a dibber or pencil roughly to the same depth as the seedlings were planted in their old pot or seed tray.*

2 *Place the seedling carefully into the hole, leaving a little of the old compost around the roots to prevent damage, and gently firm the earth around the plant to prevent air pockets.*

Potting on

❀ As the plants grow, they will need more space for the roots to grow uncramped, and will need more nutrients from the soil. The subsequent container needs to be big enough to allow a generous layer of new compost to be placed around the existing rootball, but it should not be too oversized, as this will not encourage good root formation.

❀ Allow the plant to dry out slightly before transplanting, so that it may be easily removed from its container with minimal root disturbance. Fill the new pot with a layer of drainage material and new potting compost. Tap it to remove air pockets and plant at the same depth as before, filling in with compost carefully and firming in gently. Water well and leave to drain.

SOWING OUTDOORS

Hardy perennials and annuals are generally sown directly into the soil in their desired final positions, avoiding any need for transplanting later. This is a particularly useful technique for growing deep tap-rooted plants such as poppies, which do not transplant well. Sowing usually takes place in spring, after the risk of frost has passed and when the soil has warmed, so that the seeds do not rot.

❀ However, precise sowing times will depend on when and where the plants are to flower, and the temperatures they need for germination. For example, some hardy biennials, which are also sown outside, grow quickly and should not be sown until midsummer, while others are slow starters and need to be sown in late spring. Always read seed packets carefully before sowing, and be sympathetic to the requirements of particular seed types best growing success.

❀ There are two methods for sowing outdoors – broadcast and drill sowing. In drill sowing, the seeds are sown in rows. Broadcast sowing is literally casting the seeds broadly on the seedbed where they are to grow. Both types of sowing need to be on properly prepared soil for the best possible chance of success.

The seedbed

❀ Ideally, you will be sowing into a bed that has been dug over the previous autumn, and which benefited from the addition of some mature organic matter at the same time – roughly 1 cu m (1$\frac{1}{3}$ cu yd) of organic matter to every 4 cu m (5$\frac{1}{4}$ cu yd) of soil. You do not want to sow seed into an overly rich soil, as this will encourage the production of foliage rather than flowers.

❀ If, however, you know that you are sowing into very poor soil, you may fork in a fertiliser dressing at the rate of approximately 60 g per sq m (2 oz per sq yd). If your soil is particularly heavy, you may wish to incorporate grit or coarse sand to open it up and improve drainage.

WATERING PROPAGATED PLANTS

Seedlings need careful watering to encourage growth after sowing outdoors.

1 *To water a large area, connect up a hosepipe to the mains water supply. Choose a pipe with a very fine rose.*

2 *Begin to water the area, preventing the soil from becoming waterlogged and rinsing out all the nutrients. Move on to the next area and repeat.*

BROADCAST SOWING

1 *Tread the soil evenly to produce a firm, even surface. Rake the soil to remove stones and retain a level surface with a fine, crumbly texture, so that the seeds have a good opportunity to gain direct overall contact with the soil.*

2 *Sow the seeds finely and evenly over the prepared area. Very fine seeds may be mixed with sand to produce a more consistent spread.*

3 *Rake in the seeds very lightly, working at right angles, first one way, then the other, so that they suffer only minimal disturbance.*

4 *Label the area, and water the seed using a watering can with a fine rose.*

Drill sowing

✿ In drill sowing, shallow drills, or rows, are marked out with the corner of a hoe or a trowel tip. The seeds are sown equally spaced along these rows, beneath a fine layer of soil, and are gently watered in and labelled.

✿ Drill sowing has the advantage that, since the seedlings grow in recognisable rows, it is easier to distinguish desirable plants from emerging weed seedlings. Generally, both drill-sown and broadcast-sown seeds will need thinning out.

Thinning out

✿ To prevent overcrowding, and the attendant problems as plants fight for air, light and nutrients, most seedlings will need to be thinned out as they grow.

Working when the soil is moist and the weather is mild, remove surplus seedlings, particularly the weaker, less healthy-looking specimens.

✿ Take care to press gently on to the soil around the seedlings as you work, to minimise root disturbance to those seedlings that are remaining in place.

✿ If the seedlings have grown very densely, you may need to dig up entire clumps and gently separate out healthy seedlings before replanting.

✿ Surplus seedlings can be used to bulk out sparse areas where germination was poor or sowing was patchy. They can also be planted elsewhere in the garden, as well as making wonderful offerings to gardening friends. Firm in transplanted seedlings gently, and lightly water in to settle their roots.

GROWING FROM CUTTINGS

TAKING cuttings from plant stems to produce new plants is a popular way of adding to your stocks at minimal cost. It is a good way of producing additional plants from a parent plant that is of dubious hardiness, and is an economical way of introducing a plant to your own garden that you may have admired in a friend's plot. Many gardening friendships grow alongside the developing cuttings.

❀ Stem cuttings are loosely divided into three groups, according to the season the cutting is taken, and the maturity of the parent plant. Individual plants respond to different cutting techniques, and it is wise to research the needs of a particular plant before attempting its propagation by taking cuttings. As a rough guide, perennials and small shrubs are propagated by softwood cuttings, while trees, roses and many shrubs are propagated by semi-ripe and hardwood cuttings. Once you know which technique a plant prefers, the basic techniques of taking and rooting cuttings are very straightforward.

❀ There are some general rules that apply to all cuttings. Cut only from healthy plants, and take cuttings from non-flowering side shoots, as these generally root more easily than cuttings taken from the main stem. Always use a clean, sharp knife to avoid damaging plant tissue.

TAKING A STEM-TIP CUTTING

1 *Take the cutting from the parent plant then cut straight across the stem, just below a node, so that the cutting is approximately 7.5 cm (3 in) long.*

2 *Gently remove the leaves from the lower half of the cutting. Dip the base of the cutting in hormone rooting powder.*

3 *Make a hole in a container of cuttings compost, using a dibber or pencil, and insert the cutting. Gently firm and water it in.*

4 *Create a warm, humid environment by supporting a clear plastic bag above the cutting, not allowing it to touch the leaves, or place the cutting in a propagator. Keep in bright light, but not direct sunlight. Inspect daily for signs of disease or dryness and act accordingly. Pot on when the cuttings has rooted – roughly two to three weeks.*

TAKING A SOFTWOOD CUTTING

1 *From the parent plant, cut a young, vigorous side shoot approximately 10 cm (4 in) long, trimming it straight across, just below a leaf joint.*

2 *Gently remove the leaves from the lower half of the cutting. Dip the base of the cutting into hormone rooting powder.*

3 *Make a hole in the cuttings compost with a dibber or pencil and insert the cutting, firming it in gently with the dibber and ensuring that there are no air pockets around it.*

4 *Gently water in the cutting and cover with a clear plastic bag suspended above the plant on canes or wires so that it does not touch the foliage and cause it to rot.*

❀ Plant the cutting as soon as possible after taking it, and ensure that it has excellent all-round contact with the compost when planted. As with all propagation techniques, use compost, containers and utensils that are scrupulously clean to avoid the risk of plant infection. You may wish to water in with sterilised water mixed with fungi cide for added protection. Do not check that plants have rooted by tugging at the cuttings impatiently. The best method is to look out for new growth instead.

Stem-tip cuttings

❀ Herbaceous perennials that do not divide well are often grown by the stem-tip method. Cuttings may be taken at any time during the growing season, assuming that suitable shoots are available. These need to be healthy and sturdy, with no flower buds. Plant the cuttings as soon as possible after collection.

Softwood cuttings

❀ Softwood cuttings are cuttings of the current season's growth, taken from early spring through to midsummer. Generally, they are literally soft, immature tissue, green from tip to base and, as such, wilt quickly after cutting. If propagating by this method, speed and care when collecting are of the essence. Collect the cuttings in a closed plastic bag, kept away from sunlight.

❀ Prepare the cuttings as soon as possible after collection for the best chance of success. Some softwood cuttings root readily in water, while others need to be put into compost. Research the particular requirements of the plant you are propagating. Some will need the heat from beneath, provided by a propagator or heated mat, for rooting. Some may be placed in a cold frame. As when germinating seeds, keep the cuttings in a well-lit but not directly sunny position.

❀ Once you have planted the cuttings, check the pot or propagator on alternate days to see if water is needed. Most softwood cuttings root in approximately six to eight weeks. When new growth appears, the plant may be gradually hardened off.

Semi-ripe cuttings

❀ Semi-ripe cuttings are also taken from the current season's growth, but are cut later in the year – from midsummer through to early autumn. Again, choose non-flowering, healthy side shoots. These should be soft at the top and just hard at the base.

❀ Because they are slightly harder than softwood cuttings, semi-ripe cuttings are not so susceptible to wilt. However, they do take longer to root, and for this reason they are often propagated

from heel cuttings, which means they have the base of the stem 'wounded' to encourage rooting.

❀ Wounding involves making a shallow cut, approximately 2.5–3.5 cm (1–1½ in) up from the base of the cutting, and stripping away the bark from this point to the base, using a sharp knife, not tearing away the bark. Root production is then stimulated from the wounded edge as well as the base of the cutting. Heel cuttings expose the swollen base of the season's growth, which contains a concentration of growth hormones, thereby assisting rooting.

TAKING A HEEL CUTTING

1 *Pull off a strong, non-flowering side shoot from the parent plant, pulling outwards and downwards so that you bring away a small heel of bark. Tug sharply, rather than peeling the heel cutting away. Take care not to strip away bark from the parent plant, as this could encourage infection.*

2 *Using a clean, sharp knife, cut off the leaves from the lower half of the cutting's stem. Trim away any excess, damaged plant tissue and any long tails of bark.*

3 *Dip the bottom 2.5 cm (1 in) of the cutting into hormone rooting powder. This helps prevent fungicidal attack, as well as assisting rooting.*

4 *Dib a planting hole in a small pot of cuttings compost. Gently firm in and water in the cutting. Cover the pot with a clear plastic bag, suspended*

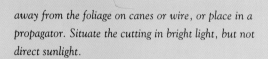

away from the foliage on canes or wire, or place in a propagator. Situate the cutting in bright light, but not direct sunlight.

Hardwood cuttings

❀ Many shrubs can be raised from hardwood cuttings. These are taken from ripe, vigorous, current season's growth – from mid-autumn to early winter. Hardwood cuttings from deciduous shrubs are taken just after the leaves have fallen.

❀ Cuttings propagated in this way are slow to root but, well cared for, will produce strong, resilient plants in about a year. Propagate hardwood cuttings in containers, in a cold frame, or even in open ground.

❀ To grow cuttings on, dip the end of the cutting into hormone rooting powder. Dib a planting hole and plant in cuttings compost in a container. Firm and water in gently. Label and place pots in a cold frame. Water well during the growing season. Harden off before planting out.

TAKING A HARDWOOD CUTTING

1 *Take pencil-thick cuttings at the junction of the current, and last season's growth.*

2 *Trim the cuttings to approximately 15 cm (6 in) lengths. At the top, cut just above buds or leaves, and at the base, cut just below buds or leaves. Make an angled cut at the top, cut straight across at the bottom – you will then know which way up to plant the cutting.*

3 *Remove any remaining deciduous leaves. On evergreen cuttings, remove leaves from the lower two-thirds of the stem and cut large leaves in half across.*

4 *If propagating outside, plant cuttings 15 cm (6 in) apart, in a trench 15 cm (6 in) deep filled with compost and sharp sand. Back fill with soil, and water in. Firm the soil after heavy frosts and water during periods of drought.*

DIVIDING PLANTS

DIVIDING plants not only regenerates what might have become quite a sad-looking plant, but is also an incredibly easy and cost-effective way of increasing your plant stocks. Many perennials will deteriorate over time, slowly dying out in the centre, unless they are lifted and divided every three or four years.

❀ Division entails literally splitting the old plant into lots of smaller sections, the most healthy of which are replanted. Large divisions made in spring may even flower later in the season – albeit initially with shorter stems than the original, established plants.

❀ If the size difference between the young plants and their neighbours in the border bothers you, plant the new sections in pots or nursery beds until they are of a suitable size to put in their new positions.

Where to begin

❀ Left to their own devices, most plants reproduce themselves anyway. Propagation by division, complex as it may sound, simply involves the gardener taking a more active part in a natural process.

❀ Most gardeners start by dividing perennials since it is usually a reproachfully sad-looking border plant, dying out in the middle and straggly around the edges, that

DIVIDING RHIZOMES

1 *Carefully remove the clump from the ground with a fork, taking care to insert the fork well away from the rhizomes as you do not damage them. Shake away any excess soil.*

2 *Roughly break up the clump with your hands or a fork. Large clumps may need the back-to-back fork technique used on large perennials. Detach fresh new rhizomes using a clean, sharp knife. Each piece should have buds or leaves above it and roots below it. Discard diseased or old rhizomes.*

3 *Trim back long roots by one-third. On irises, cut the leaves into a mitred shape, approximately 15 cm (6 in) long to avoid damage by wind rock. Dust the cut edges of the rhizome with hormone rooting powder to help prevent disease and to encourage new growth.*

4 *Plant the new rhizomes at the same depth at which they were originally growing, their leaves and buds upright. Water and firm in.*

provokes some activity. Rather than simply discarding the whole plant, it is well worth taking some healthy sections from the outside of the plant, and producing many healthy, young plants from the single old specimen.

When to divide

❀ Be aware that some plants resent disturbance, so always check the needs of a particular plant before dividing it. Division usually takes place in the semi-dormant seasons early spring or autumn – on a day when the soil is moist but not waterlogged.

❀ Some plants have a marked preference for the time of year that they are moved, however, so again, research carefully before moving plants. Rhizomes (plants with fleshy, almost horizontal underground stems), such as bergenias, rhizomatous lilies and rhizomatous irises, are very easy to divide and are generally divided in the late summer.

DIVIDING PERENNIALS

1 *Dig up the overcrowded clump with a fork, disturbing the roots as little as possible. Shake off excess soil locate the best points for division. Discard diseased parts, as well as the central part of the plant. Divisions from the outer section of the clump will grow into new, healthy plants. Wash away excess soil with water if you cannot see the roots and shoots clearly enough for accurate division.*

2 *Divide the plant into sections that have healthy roots and shoots. You divide some plants with your hands, but plants with fleshy, tough roots will need to be cut with a clean, sharp knife. Dust any cuts with fungicide, following the manufacturer's directions.*

3 *Very tough, fibrously rooted clumps may need to be divided using two forks placed back to back in the centre of the clump, to provide additional separation and leverage. Hand forks will suffice in some cases; full size garden forks may be needed in others. Always ease the forks apart gently, teasing out the roots to separate them, rather than wrenching them violently apart and breaking the roots.*

4 *Replant the new plant sections immediately after division, at the same depth at which they were already planted, with the roots spread well out. Firm in and water in well.*

Dividing bulbs

❀ After one or two seasons in the soil, most bulbs and corms produce offsets around their base. The offsets of bulbs are known as daughter bulbs; tiny ones are called bulblets. Corm offsets are known as cormels or cormlets. If these are allowed to develop unabated, they become overcrowded and compete for nutrients. The result, in most cases, is a dramatic reduction in flowering.

❀ It is therefore a good idea to lift and divide most clumps of bulbs and corms every three or four years, to sustain a really good show. Apart from preventing overcrowding, propagating bulbs also enables you to increase your flowering display at no cost, and with relatively little effort. Since the bulbs are increasing themselves naturally below the ground, it is simplicity itself to separate the developing bulbs from the parents and increase your stocks.

❀ Most popular bulbs and corms, for example narcissi, snowdrops, crocuses and lilies, will respond extremely well to division. Flowering will be increased and you will be able to plant over a wider area with your additional numbers of bulbs or corms. However, it is highly recommended that you check each plant's individual preference before planning division, as there are a few exceptions to these rules. For example, the Scarborough lily (*Vallota*) flowers well when overcrowded, while the autumn daffodil (*Sternbergia*) and cyclamens hate disturbance.

When to divide bulbs and corms

❀ Dividing is best done when the plant is dormant. However, it is obviously much easier to locate the bulbs when they have visible foliage, so division is usually undertaken when the leaves have almost entirely died down. Some bulbs have slightly different needs. For example, snowdrops are best divided when they are in full leaf, so again check each plant's individual requirements before you begin.

DIVIDING BULBS

1 *Gently lift the clump with a fork.*

2 *Shake off the excess soil and separate the clump into smaller, more manageable portions.*

3 *Pull away the individual bulbs with your hands. Discard soft, dried out, damaged or diseased bulbs.*

Clean the bulbs that you wish to replant, removing any loose tunics (the papery membrane enveloping bulbs).

4 *Plant the offset bulbs at the correct depth and spacing in prepared soil. This is generally between two and three times the size of the bulb, but check the requirements of the individual species before dividing.*

INCREASING BULBS BY SCORING

Towards the end of the dormant season, hyacinths may be increased by scoring.

1 *Use a sharp knife to make cuts through the basal plate of the bulb. Dust the cut areas with fungicide and store the bulb in damp perlite, mixed with fungicide, in a warm place. The injury caused by the cutting will encourage small bulbs (bulblets) to develop along the cuts.*

2 *When bulblets have formed, plant the bulb upside down in gritty compost. The bulblets will grow above the parent bulb and may be carefully separated from the old bulb for replanting. A simpler method is to score the parent bulb, plant it again immediately and wait for bulblets to form.*

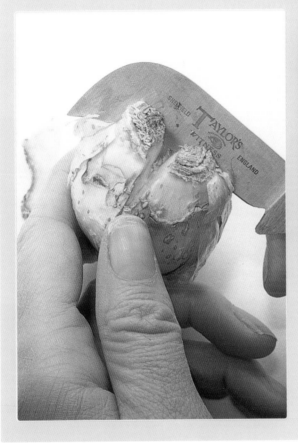

Scaling bulbs

❀ Scaling is a straightforward method for increasing the stocks of bulbs that consist of scales, most notably lilies, which are quite simple to propagate in this way. Propagating lilies is particularly satisfying since the bulbs are comparatively expensive to buy. A bonus is that, after scaling, the parent lily may be replanted to continue flowering as normal.

❀ Most lily bulbs comprise concentric rings of scales, joined at their bases to a basal plate. To scale lilies, work in early autumn, before root growth begins. Lift the bulbs, or scrape away soil from around the bulb and work *in situ*. Remove a few scales from the bulb, taking care to remove a little of the basal plate tissue when you detach the scales. This will greatly increase your chances of success.

❀ Coat the scales with fungicide and place them in a tray of two parts damp peat substitute and one part coarse sand. Keep them moist in a warm, shaded place for approximately two months. In spring, move them to a cold place for two months, to encourage good leaf development. Pot on the single bulblets and grow on for another year before planting out.

LAYERING

LAYERING offers the novice gardener a superb introduction to propagation, since the young plants are not separated from the parent plant until they have formed roots and are growing independently. This is obviously not as challenging as raising plants from seed or cuttings, where the new plants are very vulnerable until established and need particular care to ensure strong rooting and vigorous growth, and require vigilant attention to ensure disease is kept at bay.

❁ Layering is such a simple propagation method that some plants even layer themselves, for example strawberry plants and shrubs with low branches like the smoke bush (*Cotinus coggygria*). Others attempt to layer naturally (self-layering plants), and can be easily encouraged in their efforts by pegging or weighing down branches until they root.

❁ Many climbers, such as ivy, have trailing shoots that develop roots on contact with the soil. The propagation in this case has already taken place. All you need do is gently ease the new plant from the soil without damaging the roots, and cut it away from the main stem before replanting the new plant.

❁ Layering is also a very useful technique for increasing stocks of plants, such as some shrubs and climbers, that do not root easily from cuttings. Layering is not necessarily a rapid propagation method, but the plants produced are strong, already well adapted to the soil in which they are to grow to maturity, and the technique is not labour intensive.

❁ In addition, it needs no specialist equipment, can be done at any time of the year, and does not take up any space on your windowsill or in a greenhouse. Thus, every gardener could start their propagation experience with a little layering.

❁ There are essentially three types of layering: air layering, where the growing medium is brought up to the plant stem; a range of techniques where soil is mounded over a stem, for example French, trench and stool layering; and the basic range of techniques in which the stem is brought down into the soil, namely tip, serpentine, natural and simple layering.

❁ This is all easier than it sounds, and most amateur gardeners will find the last techniques mentioned, which capitalise on the plant's own desire to root when it reaches the soil, sufficient for their propagation needs.

Planting self-layered climbers

❁ You may spot several places along a trailing stem where the plant has taken root. It is easy to see where the stems have produced new root systems as there is abundant healthy young growth at these points.

❁ Gently ease these areas of the stem away from the ground, bringing the roots up carefully. Using sharp secateurs, cut away this section of stem from the parent plant. Cut the stem into sections, each with a good root system. Remove any leaves growing close to the rooted areas. Plant each portion of rooted stem in compost or directly in the garden, watering in well.

BELOW: *As the shoots of ivies (such as this* Hedera helix *'Goldheart') tend to produce roots naturally when they come into contact with the soil, the propagation is already done.*

INCREASING PLANTS BY LAYERING

1 *Although many plants layer themselves, some will benefit from a helping hand. Choose a healthy, flexible stem that may be easily bent to touch the soil. Cut off any side shoots.*

2 *Make a shallow hole in the ground at an appropriate point, and enrich the area with compost. For an increased chance of success, make a short slanting cut on the underside of the stem at the point where it is to be layered. The concentration of carbohydrates and hormones at the point of the wound, together with the plant being slightly stressed in the area, helps to promote root growth.*

3 *Twist the shoot to open the cut. Apply hormone rooting powder to the injured part, to discourage disease and further encourage rooting.*

4 *Place the injured part of the stem in the soil and secure it firmly with a metal peg or piece of bent wire, making sure that the cut remains open. Backfill with soil, firm and water in using a watering can fitted with a fine rose. Keep the area moist throughout the growing season. After about a year, scrape away the soil to check for new roots. If all is well, sever the new plant from the parent and leave it in situ to establish for another season before moving it to its final site.*

PRUNING PLANTS

Pruning describes the act of cutting away unwanted growth – unwanted because it is diseased, old, or simply in the way. It is a subject that many gardeners find daunting. Individual plants have individual pruning needs, which means that any book covering pruning necessarily contains a large amount of information. Do not be put off by this. Once you understand the chief principles of pruning, together with the pruning requirements specific to the plants in your own garden, you will be equipped to enhance dramatically the look and health of many plants.

ABOVE: *Renovating a neglected plant by pruning is a simple yet very satisfying task.*

THE USES OF PRUNING

PRUNING can maintain a balance between growth and flowering. It can restrict growth, which may be necessary should a plant encroach on a walkway or into a neighbour's garden. It can train plants, encouraging a neat habit and profuse flowering or fruiting. Pruning can also help to maintain healthy plants, with good-quality stems, foliage, fruit and flowers.

❀ Pruning falls loosely into three categories – renovative, regenerative and formative pruning.

RENOVATIVE PRUNING

There are a number of specific conditions that can be treated or prevented by pruning.

Rubbing or crossing shoots

❀ Where shoots repeatedly rub against each other, they will eventually become damaged by friction, forming open wounds that expose the plant to disease spores. Crossing shoots also look untidy and prevent the plant from growing into a pleasing overall shape.

Removing dieback

❀ When young shoots die back towards the main stem, you need to cut them out. Otherwise dieback can continue unabated, affecting healthy tissue, too. To prevent this spread, prune back as far as the healthy part of the stem, cutting just above a bud.

Halting disease

❀ Cut out rot and disease before they spread and affect the rest of the plant. Remove dead shoots, as these not only harbour disease, but also look unattractive. Cut back as far as healthy wood.

Pruning to retain variegation

❀ Pruning is also used to prevent variegated plants from reverting – that is, becoming plain once more. If you see mature green leaves appearing on an otherwise variegated plant, cut them back to the point of origin, as they will tend to grow vigorously and gradually dominate

RENOVATIVE PRUNING

Renovative pruning is pruning to remove problems such as damaged and diseased parts of a plant. It is always preferable to prune to avoid problems in advance, rather than after they have occurred. Careful pruning can help stop plant troubles before they begin. For example, pruning to keep the plant uncongested, allows plenty of light and air to travel through the plant, keeping it growing well and discouraging pests and diseases.

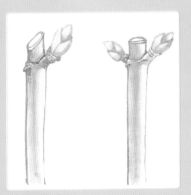

ABOVE: *Two examples of correct pruning; on the single shoot the cut is angled away from the bud; on the double shoot, the distance of the cut from the buds is just right.*

ABOVE: *Example of cutting incorrectly, from left to right: too far away, too close, with blunt secateurs, or sloping towards a bud. Bad techniques cause plant problems such as dieback, rotting and disease.*

the plant. Some plants develop variegated leaves only as the foliage matures, so check the individual characteristics of your plant and wait until you are certain before pruning.

REGENERATIVE PRUNING

Some plants benefit enormously from hard, yearly pruning. Plants such as dogwoods and willows require this heavy pruning so that they will produce strong, large leaves and healthy, colourful new stems. Other plants, notably shrub roses and fruit, grow much more vigorously and flower more profusely, with better-quality blooms, if pruned annually.

FORMATIVE PRUNING

Formative pruning is literally pruning so as to achieve and maintain a desirable form. It is always preferable to start creating the desired form early on in a plant's life, rather than trying to impose a shape on a plant once it has been allowed to grow unchecked for a long time.

PRUNING TECHNIQUES

ABOVE: *Removing badly crossing shoots encourages good air circulation throughout the plant.*

ABOVE: *Pruning variegated plants is vital to stop them reverting, in which case plain leaves will soon dominate the plant.*

ABOVE: *Cut out dieback and damaged stems, which may otherwise cause infection and continue to die back.*

ABOVE: *Remove rotten stems, which could cause disease throughout the plant.*

PRUNING BASICS

CARELESS pruning can do more harm than good. It is critically important that you do not damage the plant when pruning. Use clean, sharp tools, and respect the natural growth pattern of the plant.

❁ For plants with leaves that grow alternately up the stem, cut at an angle, approximately 5 mm (¼ in) above an outward-facing bud. Make sure that the cut slopes away from the bud so that moisture runs away from it, not towards it, which would encourage rot.

❁ For plants with leaves that grow in pairs, cut straight across, just above a pair of buds.

❁ In both cases, you need to cut quite close to the buds, as stem tissue heals much better close to growth buds. If the cut is too high, the stem will probably die back to the bud, which renders the plant susceptible to disease, and also looks unsightly. Conversely, do not cut right up against the bud, as you could damage the bud itself, or introduce infection.

❁ Always make a clean, sharp cut. A ragged cut or a bruised, torn stem is very prone to disease.

PRUNING TREES

THE individual requirements of a tree must be taken into account before pruning. Some trees will require minimal pruning or may even be harmed by pruning, for example the mulberry tree, while others, like tree of heaven (Ailanthus), will relish hard pruning in order to check growth and produce luxuriant foliage.

Evergreen trees

❁ Evergreens are generally pruned in late spring, but always check the individual needs of your particular evergreen before you prune.

❁ With young trees, train the main or leader stem upwards to establish a strong main stem and a good basic form for the tree. Prune out leader shoots that are competing with each other, as well as badly crossing or rubbing stems.

❁ Mature evergreens need little pruning, apart from removing any dead, damaged or diseased branches. Cut back to a healthy shoot or remove the offending branch altogether. Remove crossing lateral shoots and competing leader shoots. Do not be tempted to simply hack away at the top of a conifer that is too tall, as this can leave a very ugly shape. If possible, dig up the tree and start again.

Deciduous trees

❁ Most deciduous trees are pruned when dormant, in late autumn or winter. However, as always, check the individual requirements of your tree before pruning, since some trees need to be pruned in spring or summer.

❁ The aim of pruning and training a young tree is to produce an attractive and stable framework. The central stem should be straight, and the branches nicely spaced. It is particularly important to prune trees that bud in pairs, such as ash. If the central stem is allowed to develop into a fork, it may even split. Other trees, if allowed to fork too soon, will not have an attractive overall shape.

❁ To create a vertical stem on an ornamental tree remove competing shoots, as well as weak or crossing laterals. Remove all lateral shoots from the bottom third of the tree in the first spring after planting, and reduce the lateral shoots in the middle section of the tree by about half. In late autumn/early winter completely remove the lateral shoots on the middle section that you reduced in the spring. Continue this process over the next two years until you have produced a vertical stem reaching approximately 2 m (7 ft) in height.

Mature deciduous trees

❁ Established deciduous trees should need little pruning, other than to maintain the pleasing shape that has hopefully been created over the years. Remove congested branches from the centre of the tree, as these will block light and air flow. Retain the overall shape of the tree by removing any branches that have become too dominant and unsightly.

BELOW: This elegant, sweeping avenue of trees should now only need pruning to keep the pleasing shape created by expert management over the years.

PRUNING ORNAMENTAL TREES

There are basic rules for pruning young ornamental trees, but check on the individual requirements of each plant first.

cut the leader
back to a
strong bud

1 *Three years after planting, cut the leader back
to a strong lateral or bud, 30 cm (12 in) above the
required length of clear stem.*

allow unchecked
growth in
summer of
fourth year

2 *During the summer of the fourth year,
allow laterals and sublaterals to develop
without pruning.*

prune out
crossing or
crowded laterals
and sublaterals

3 *In the autumn of the fourth year, prune out crossing
or crowded laterals and sublaterals to leave between
three and five evenly spaced laterals.*

remove branches
that spoil the
symmetry of
the tree

4 *In the fifth and subsequent years, remove young
branches that spoil the tree's symmetry, as well as
shoots that appear on the main stem.*

POLLARDING AND COPPICING

POLLARDING describes the act of pruning a tree back to its main stem, so as to produce new shoots at this point. Coppicing, similarly, involves the regular pruning of a tree close to the ground. Both techniques were traditionally employed to produce accessible and regular supplies of pliable wood for firewood, fence and basket making. Nowadays, coppicing and pollarding are generally done to produce colourful stems, or to restrict the size of a tree.

❀ Both pollarding and coppicing are generally done in late winter or early spring. When the trunk has reached the desired height, cut the branches back to approximately 5 cm (2 in) away from the main stem. This brutal-looking treatment will encourage a mass of new shoots to be produced during the summer. Ideally, repeat the process annually, and feed and mulch the tree after pruning.

Cutting large branches

❀ The pruning of very large, mature trees is best dealt with by professional arborists. There may be judicial constraints on cutting certain trees in certain situations, so always check the legal position before planning major work on mature trees.

❀ Smaller trees, or overgrown old shrubs may have thickish branches that you are able to remove yourself safely. Use a pruning saw and cut in three stages, starting with an upward cut, so that the weight of the branch does not cause it to rip away from the plant in a ragged, uncontrolled way.

PRUNING SHRUBS

THE general rules and reasons for pruning trees apply equally to shrubs. Some shrubs require virtually no pruning other than a light 'haircut', but the majority will eventually deteriorate if they are left unpruned. For most shrubs, pruning will naturally encourage strong, healthy growth and vigorous flowering with well-sized, good-quality blooms.

❀ As a rule, flowering shrubs are pruned soon after the last of their flowers have died off. There are notable exceptions, however, such as some late summer-flowering shrubs like buddleja and hydrangea, which would be susceptible to frost damage if pruned at this time. Wait until spring before pruning these. As always, for best results, always check the individual requirements of a shrub before planning pruning.

Hard pruning

❀ Hard pruning on the right sort of shrub can produce really rewarding results. Tall, straggly flowering shrubs are a depressingly common sight in front gardens everywhere – mean, spindly stems topped with a few, small flowers that are so high they are not even at eye level where they can be enjoyed.

❀ Ideally, plan your shrub's pruning needs while the plant is still young, starting your pruning programme the first year after planting. It is always preferable to create and maintain a good pruning routine, rather than to attempt to resuscitate a shrub that may have become unhealthy, out of shape and congested as a result of having been left unpruned for many years.

❀ You can try cutting this sort of neglected shrub back to just above ground level, as it may produce basal shoots, but the results are not predictable. Most hard pruning is done in spring, to encourage vigorous growth, but always check the individual requirements of any shrub before

HOW TO POLLARD AND COPPICE TREES

Pollarding and coppicing are generally done to provide colourful stems or to restrict the size of a tree. Both methods promote healthy regrowth.

ABOVE: *Pollarding means cutting stems hard back to the trunk to produce vigorous new shoots.*

ABOVE: *Coppicing involves pruning back almost to ground level to encourage basal shoots to develop.*

HOW TO PRUNE SHRUBS

As with trees, it is important to understand the requirements of each indvidual shrub to avoid inflicting heavy damage or not getting the best out of a shrub by pruning too lightly.

ABOVE: *Hard pruning is advisable only for certain shrubs. It stimulates vigorous new growth and encourages a good floral display on appropriate plants.*

ABOVE: *Ungainly shrubs can be persuaded into more pleasing shapes by careful pruning, which provides a better framework of stems.*

ABOVE: *Some shrubs, like this dogwood (Cornus), are pruned hard in spring to produce colourful stems.*

pruning, since pruning at the correct time of year is of crucial importance.

❀ Hard pruning seems very drastic, but on shrubs that flower on shoots produced in the current year, it is easy to see how, left unpruned, the stems would simply continue to grow, with the flowers appearing at the very ends only. You will need to cut back all the previous summer's growth to within approximately 5 cm (2 in) of last year's stem. Although the result looks brutal, the plant will generate healthy new shoots at this point.

❀ Cut back to a point just above a bud, outward facing if possible, to give the plant a good overall shape. In general, cut the plant back as far as new growth, but to regenerate a very bushy old shrub that has become crowded and out of shape, cut a few stems back almost to ground level to improve the overall shape.

Deadheading

❀ Many plants, such as heathers and lavenders, need deadheading as soon as the flowers have died back. Check if each plant needs deadheading before doing so automatically, as there are a few exceptions.

❀ Using shears, trim away the dead blooms to a point just below the flower spike. Take care not to cut into the old wood, as some shrubs do not flower well, or at all, on old wood, and you will be left with unattractive bare brown areas if you cut too enthusiastically.

BELOW: *Pruning shrubs at the right time will help to increase flower production next season.*

PRUNING CLIMBERS

CLIMBERS grow in several different ways. Clinging climbers such as ivy attach themselves to their supports by aerial roots or suckers, and do not require a supplementary support systems like trellis.

❀ Twining climbers, such as honeysuckle and clematis, entwine around a support by means of tendrils, stems or leaf stalks, and benefit from a support. Scrambling plants, for example some types of rose, hang on using hooked thorns. Scrambling, rambling plants will need tying on to a support. A guide to pruning scrambling climbers is given in the section on pruning roses that follows. For pruning twining climbers, see the section on pruning clematis.

Basic principles

❀ Climbers have different pruning needs, depending on their flowering season and the age of the wood on which they flower. As a guide, climbers that flower on the previous season's growth need pruning when flowering has finished. Climbers that flower on the current season's growth are pruned in early spring or at the end of winter, so that they have adequate time to produce new flowering shoots.

❀ Having checked that you are pruning at the right time of year for the plant concerned, there are general rules to follow for all pruning. Use sharp tools and make clean cuts, removing damaged or weak growth.

❀ Cut out branches that are rubbing, or that have become congested. Prune just above a bud or healthy shoot; on climbers that grow in an opposite-facing pattern, cut straight across above a pair of buds. On climbers that grow with an alternating pattern, make a cut that slopes away, just above a bud pointing in the direction that you want the new shoot to develop.

Pruning to control growth

❀ Although clinging climbers are easy to grow and establish, they can overwhelm a structure. Ivy, in particular, can inflict severe structural damage. Roots can penetrate mortar and, as plant stems thicken, guttering can be forced away from the building.

ABOVE: *Vigorous climbers, such as honeysuckle, need careful pruning to keep them in check.*

❀ Vigorous climbers like this can creep under and loosen roof tiles and wooden cladding. Once they have taken hold, removal is difficult, so it is important to keep a watchful annual pruning eye on these plants to ensure a balance between attractively cloaking growth and unwelcome invasion. Remove as much growth as you need, at the time of year appropriate to the plant.

RIGHT: *To retain a well-shaped, wall-trained climber, prune and train diligently from the start.*

Pruning for good coverage

❀ Pruning clinging climbers early in their life also promotes an even growth pattern with a well-spaced framework of new shoots. Although self-clinging climbers do not technically need tying in and supporting, they will grow to cover a surface more evenly if trained laterally while still young and pliable and pruned to encourage budding from side shoots.

❀ In order to do this successfully, you should either tie or peg down the young stems. In the second spring after planting, cut back the plant's side shoots to a point just above a bud near the main stem. As each new stem develops, cut back the tip the next year so that the shoots branch out and create better coverage of the support. Cut back other new shoots to within two buds of the nearest stem.

RENOVATING NEGLECTED CLIMBERS

A NEGLECTED climber is a rather depressing sight. Not only does the plant bulge unattractively from its support, but it may start to pull the support away from the wall or fence altogether.

❀ Neighbouring plants may be forced into deep shade, affecting their growth adversely, too. A tangled, congested mass of mostly dead or dying stems can be a daunting prospect. However, tackle it with confidence, since, in most cases, even severely overgrown climbers can be regenerated with appropriate pruning.

❀ Some climbers will grow again even if cut back almost to the base. As with all pruning, check the individual needs of your plant before picking up the secateurs. If the plant's ability to withstand drastic pruning is uncertain, tackle renovative pruning over a two-year period.

❀ Gradually, fresh, vigorous growth will replace what you have removed. Be methodical if you are undertaking renovative pruning over a protracted period; otherwise, new shoots will grow and become entwined with the old stems, which will make pruning extremely difficult.

❀ Although the plant will look unbalanced during this time, it is best to cut down one side of the plant only in the first year of renovation. A very neglected plant may take several years to recover from this treatment, so do not be hasty to dismiss the success of your work if the plant does not flower for two years or so, even after both sides have been pruned. Be patient.

prune any crossing or rubbing stems, which can cause plant weakness and disease

woody stems will need lopping, rather than trimming with secateurs

remove very tangled, matted growth for a neat, healthy climber

PRUNING ROSES

ROSE stems grow and produce flowers for only a few years before becoming exhausted and starting to develop flowers lower down the stem. Pruning is therefore needed to prevent the plant becoming an ungainly tangled mass of dying and living wood, with inferior blooms.

Rambling roses

❀ Rambling roses have diminished in popularity over the years. They bloom only once a year, albeit with a spectacular show of flowers, but are not generally disease resistant, and do need regular pruning.

❀ Flowers grow on new wood, so you will need to prune each year for a good show of flowers all over the plant. However, rambling roses are a good choice in some areas, where their natural talents can be exploited. Their long, flexible stems will clamber enthusiastically up dead trees that would otherwise be an eyesore, or scramble riotously along the soil to produce unusual ground cover.

Climbing roses

❀ Climbing roses have much less flexible stems than ramblers; many are more disease resistant, and some are repeat-flowering. Since flowers develop on a framework of established wood, pruning climbers is much less demanding than pruning ramblers. Essential pruning is restricted to removing dead, weak or diseased growth.

❀ Deadhead as much as is practical during the summer, and prune in the autumn, after flowering. If you also shorten the side shoots that have flowered, taking them back to approximately three buds, you will encourage a good coverage of flowers next year.

Regenerating an old climber

❀ If a climbing rose has been neglected, and lateral growth not encouraged by regular training and tying in, there may be many bare stems visible near ground level. You can encourage new, basal shoots to develop by cutting down some of the old bare stems almost to ground level.

SHRUB AND MINIATURE ROSES

The term 'shrub rose' covers many old varieties of rose, which predate the floribundas and hybrid teas roses so popular today. Shrub roses generally have a much shorter flowering period than their contemporary rivals, and often produce much bigger bushes, so are not as popular as they once were. However, there are notable exceptions to these rules. Some shrub roses are repeat-flowering; some do grow in smaller bush sizes and some, although they do flower only once in a season, flower spectacularly and over such a long period that they are still excellent choices. Shrub roses do not generally have very demanding pruning needs, an attribute shared by miniature roses. Pruning of these roses is generally limited to controlling the size of the bush, as well as removing dead, diseased or weak growth. Miniatures may be pruned with scissors, instead of secateurs.

light pruning is not recommended, except for very vigorous hybrid tea roses

hard pruning is recommended for newly planted bush roses, and to renovate neglected plants

roses respond wonderfully to efficient pruning, producing a multitude of flowers

miniature roses only need scissors to cut off spent blooms and diseased or damaged stems

Cutting out suckers

❀ Where plants have been produced by grafting, suckers may develop. These shoots grow from the original rootstock, not the required variety grafted on to it. If left unchecked, these suckers will eventually overwhelm the plant completely, reverting it to the rootstock variety.

❀ It is vital to remove the sucker properly at its source. You will probably need to remove some soil, before pulling off the sucker where it has developed on the rootstock. If you simply snip suckers off at ground level, they will thrive on this pruning and develop even more.

Hybrid tea and floribunda roses

❀ Hybrid tea and floribunda roses are popular garden choices, and have broadly similar pruning needs.

❀ Hybrid teas have been used for around 100 years. Their flowers have what is often seen as a 'classic' rose shape. They are available in an amazing range of colours and are often well fragranced. However, there are drawbacks with some varieties.

❀ Many hybrid tea bushes are quite rigid in shape, producing a slightly stiff appearance that does not suit every garden, and hybrid teas generally bloom less frequently than floribundas. They are also more susceptible to rain damage, and are not tolerant of less-than-perfect conditions; so choose your breed carefully.

❀ Floribundas have been popular for around the last 50 years. Although the individual blooms may not be as choice as their hybrid tea counterparts,

ABOVE: *Most hybrid tea and established floribunda roses require moderate pruning.*

floribundas are chosen for their ability to flower continuously for long periods, for their increased disease resistance, their ability to thrive in less-than-ideal conditions, and for their rain tolerance.

❀ Prune these roses in early spring, when growth is just beginning, but to avoid the possibility of damage by wind rock cut back long shoots in autumn. Cut stems back to approximately half their length, and remove damaged, weak or diseased stems. For floribundas, hard prune some old stems close to the ground to encourage new basal shoots, while pruning last year's new shoots only moderately. This variable pruning will encourage a good coverage of flowers over the whole plant.

REGENERATING OLD CLIMBERS AND DEALING WITH SUCKERS

Suckers spoil the look and shape of any rose and should be dealt with firmly. Likewise, a neglected rose needs firm attention to encourage healthy and shapely regrowth.

shorten side shoots to just above a bud, facing in the direction that you want the rose to grow

when hard pruning, cut out unwanted stems close to their base for a good overall framework

remove suckers at their point of origin on the root, not at ground level

PRUNING CLEMATIS

THERE is a great deal of intimidating mystique about how to prune clematis correctly. In fact, there are just three basic methods. The choice of method appropriate for a particular clematis is the most important part of pruning this plant.

❀ Clematises are divided loosely into three groups, based on when they flower. These groups are widely referred to as Groups One, Two and Three type of clematis. When buying a new clematis, you will save yourself a lot of pruning indecision later on if you take the time to find out and note the group that your clematis falls into. Getting the type right is important. If you make a mistake in identifying the type of pruning required, you could unwittingly remove the next flush of flowers.

GROUP ONE: MINIMAL PRUNING NEEDS

THESE vigorous clematises flower in spring or early summer, directly on last season's ripened stems. They typically have quite small flowers. Clematises in this group need to be pruned hard when planted, but subsequently need only minimal pruning. If the plant becomes tangled, untidy and congested, you can prune it after flowering to control it.

❀ Popular Group One cultivars include *Clematis montana*, *C. macropetala*, *C. alpina* and *C. armandii*.

ABOVE: *Group One clematises, such as C. Montana, are very lightly pruned after flowering.*

GROUP TWO: LIGHT PRUNING NEEDS

THESE clematises produce large flowers early in summer or in midsummer. Some varieties continue flowering through into autumn. Group Two clematises flower on short stems produced in the current season, which grow on last season's ripe wood, and need only a light pruning in spring, before the plant starts active growth. Both Group One and Two clematises are sometimes referred to as 'old-wood' flowering clematis.

❀ Given their attributes of large flowers and an often prolonged flowering season, it is no wonder that Group Two contains many of the most popular hybrid clematis cultivars such as 'Nelly Moser', 'The President', 'Mrs Cholmondely' and 'Lasurstern'.

ABOVE: *Lightly prune Group Two varieties, such as 'Nelly Moser', in early spring.*

GROUP THREE: HARD PRUNING NEEDS

GROUP Three clematises flower late in the season – from mid- to late summer, and possibly through to autumn – producing blooms on the current year's stems. In early spring, before the plant starts active growth, cut back all last season's growth to just above the lowest pair of healthy buds, approximately 30 cm (12 in) above soil level. Tie in the new stems as they grow in late spring and summer. Take great care when training, as the stems are extremely brittle and prone to breakage.

❀ Group Three clematises include 'Ernest Markham', 'Jackmanii', 'Ville de Lyon', 'Perle d'Azur' and 'Gipsy Queen'.

RIGHT: *C. 'Jackmanii' and other Group Three clematises need hard pruning in early spring.*

CLEMATIS GROUPS

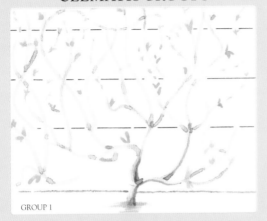

GROUP 1

ABOVE: *Prune Group 1 clematis if needed after flowering, removing a minimal amount of foliage.*

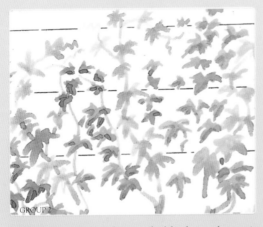

GROUP 2

ABOVE: *Prune Group 2 clematis only if the plant needs neatening up straight after flowering.*

GROUP 3

ABOVE: *Prune Group 3 clematis in late winter or early spring, taking them back to the lowest healthy shoot.*

Pruning and training clematis and other climbers on an arch or pergola

❀ Any climber looks best on a pergola or arch if it has been encouraged to produce a good, even coverage, with flowers over the whole plant, not just a few at the top, out of range of eye level. The key to producing a good climbing display is to train horizontally while the stems are flexible, and to prune main stems to encourage side shoots to develop.

❀ Always take care to tie in shoots gently, leaving room for movement and growth. Prune at the time of year appropriate for the type of clematis grown, removing diseased, damaged or dead wood. When the main shoots have climbed to the top of the support, prune them – again at the appropriate time of year – so that they do not become congested, untidy and susceptible to windrock.

BELOW: *Climbing flowering plants need careful pruning in order to keep the whole plant in bloom.*

PRUNING HEDGES

THE type of pruning a particular hedge requires depends on two things – the type of overall effect you are trying to create and the individual requirements of the plant.

❀ A dense, formal hedge like privet will need regular pruning if it is to maintain its neat good looks, whereas an informal flowering or fruiting hedge such as snowberry will need much less attention in order to achieve a desirable look.

Shaping a hedge

❀ A common mistake in trimming hedges is to produce a straight-sided form, or one that tapers towards the bottom. This will eventually yield the type of hedge that is an all-too-common sight in front gardens everywhere – the hedge that is leafy at the top and bare, twiggy and brown at the base. The reason is simple. The foliage at the base of the hedge has died due to a lack of light from being in the shade of the upper leaves and stems. Happily, there is a simple technique for preventing this.

❀ Always trim a formal hedge into a slightly pyramidal shape – so that it is approximately one-third narrower at the top than at its base – so as to allow plenty of light to reach all parts of the plant. This sloping angle also encourages greater wind resistance and helps the plant shed snow. In areas of high snowfall it may be advisable to make a more exaggerated A-shaped sloping cut at the top of the hedge, to further discourage snow from settling and ice forming on the plant.

❀ When the hedge has grown to the desired height, make yourself a cutting template from plywood to give you a clear, easy-to-follow guide to the shape and height required.

❀ When you start work from the base of the hedge, make sure that you work upwards so that clippings are discarded from the path of progress. A power trimmer makes light work of what can otherwise be an arduous task if you are dealing with hedges on a large scale. You should always use the correct safety precautions and equipment, including gloves, goggles and, if using an electric trimmer, a residual current device (RCD).

FORMAL HEDGES

Formal hedges – ones that are clipped into precise shapes – need regular trimming to maintain a good appearance. A neglected formal hedge is a very depressing sight. Just as unkempt hair on an otherwise well-dressed person gives a generally scruffy impression, an untidy formal hedge transmits an air of neglect throughout the whole garden. The aim of pruning a formal hedge is to produce a dense mass of compact shoots that will form a bushy hedge, which grows evenly within its desired shape. Clipping side shoots will remove the growing tip of each shoot to promote this bushy growth. Many formal hedges can be trimmed when they look untidy – between spring and autumn – but always check the individual pruning needs of any hedge before picking up the trimmer. Fast-growing hedges may need several cuts a year; slower growing types will look perfectly respectable with just one or two trims during that time.

a pointed top helps shrug off heavy snowfall in especially vulnerable sites

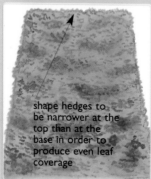

shape hedges to be narrower at the top than at the base in order to produce even leaf coverage

Informal hedges

❀ Informal hedges are much less demanding than their neatly clipped formal counterparts. They generally need pruning only once a year, and maintaining a precise finished shape is not necessary for their visual success. These hedges are generally pruned in order to control their size and spread, to cut out any disease or decay, and to encourage new shoots to appear.

❀ Pruning is usually done after the plants have flowered, but do check the needs of individual species before pruning. For example, berrying hedges are generally left unpruned until the berries have finished fruiting, or the birds have eaten them. As a rule, simply cut out any congested or weak areas, shorten old shoots and cut back some shoots almost to the ground in order to encourage basal shoots.

HEDGE-PRUNING METHODS

Decide which tools to use for cutting a hedge according to the area that needs trimming.

1 *Secateurs will suffice for lightly trimming the occasional shoot.*

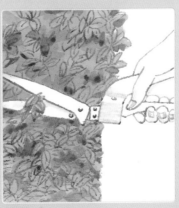

2 *Sharp shears are adequate when quite small areas of hedge need trimming.*

3 *Power tools make light work of hedge trimming. Always use the appropriate safety equipment when using power tools in the garden.*

RENOVATING A NEGLECTED HEDGE

It is tempting to ruthlessly prune a very unsightly, neglected hedge, but severe cutting can over stress the plant and recovery will be slow. Initially, working at the time of year appropriate to the plant, trim only one side hard to encourage new growth from the centre of the hedge. You may repeat this drastic pruning in the following year on the other side of the hedge, and only lightly trimming the new growth on the other side.

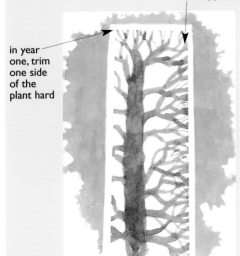

the following year, trim new growth on the opposite side

in year one, trim one side of the plant hard

MAKING A HEIGHT GUIDE

A string line gives an accurate cutting guide for trimming a formal hedge. Fix a taut, brightly coloured line at the required finished height of the hedge as an easy-to-see guide for level.

coloured string line for easy viewing

desired height of hedge

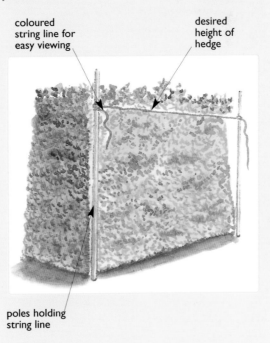

poles holding string line

TOPIARY

TOPIARY is pruning elevated to an art form. Plants have been trained and cut into artificial shapes for decorative effect since Roman times. Topiary has a place in many gardens, not only the grand, formal settings with which it is normally associated.

❀ Topiary can visually anchor a more informal setting and provide valuable, year-long structure and colour in a garden. Even the smallest garden, perhaps little more than a flight of steps leading to a doorway, can look more imposing when embellished with a neat pair of clipped, container-grown plants.

TOPIARY SHAPES

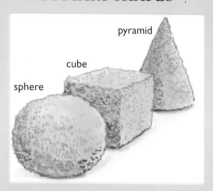

pyramid
cube
sphere

Novice topiarists are advised to start with a simple, geometric shape. Rigidly geometric shapes, such as cubes, are less forgiving of inaccurate cutting than slightly softer forms, like pyramids and spheres. More figurative shapes, such as teddy bears and peacocks, are not necessarily difficult to produce, particularly if you form them using a ready-made rigid frame as a guide. However, they can take many years to reach a size at which they can attain a recognisable shape, because the plants are generally slow growing, and are therefore not for the impatient topiarist.

Initially, young plants are snipped to shape by eye to form a loosely geometric shape. As the plant grows in subsequent years to a sufficient size, place a cutting guide over the plant and trim to shape. Canes, held together with wire at the top, make a simple and inexpensive pyramid 'template'. When the plant has reached the required shape and size, simply clip it lightly at intervals appropriate for the topiary shape and type of plant used, to maintain a crisp, outline and dense growth pattern.

❀ Low box hedging has long been used to contain herb gardens, which can, by the very nature of the plants, be quite unruly. Not only does the clipped hedging define and neaten the overall appearance of the area, but it also helps to protect the plants within its borders from the elements, and contains and intensifies the fragrance of the herbs in the local environment.

❀ Topiary can consist of very simple geometric shapes, such as spheres and cubes, or it can be extremely fanciful, such as chess pieces or a whole menagerie of animals. It can be used to add interest to a long run of hedging, or as stand-alone pieces of living sculpture. Slow-growing plants are generally chosen for topiary – species that can withstand regular clipping, but do not grow so rapidly that they lose their outline overnight.

The technique

❀ Topiary is not a low-maintenance form of pruning, although many of the plants used for topiary are chosen for their resilience and dense growth patterns. With just a little attention to some basic guidelines, successful topiary is not difficult to achieve. The results are impressive and extremely satisfying to produce.

❀ Always use very sharp, clean tools for topiary, as the soft shoots you are cutting are sappy and will be vulnerable to disease if torn. It is also very difficult to make decisive, accurate cuts on this flexible growth with blunt tools.

❀ Sheep-trimming shears are excellent for producing a light, accurate cut, but are not suitable for heavy work. Cutting little and often is the key to successful topiary. Dramatic, inexpert cutting can create an unbalanced shape, which will take at least a season to settle, and it is all too easy to cut inaccurately when making severe cuts. Cut large-leaved evergreens, such as laurel, with secateurs to prevent the unsightly halving of leaves, which can occur if clipping with shears.

Frequency of cut

❀ How frequently to clip topiary depends on the speed at which the plant grows, the intricacy of the topiary shape and the degree of finish required. Simple shapes in slow-growing plants will need relatively little clipping. For example, a yew pyramid will need only an annual trim, whereas a complex abstract geometric shape in box may need cutting at four- to six-weekly intervals during the growing season, in order to maintain its definition.

SIMPLE TOPIARY FRAMES

There is no need to buy purpose-built frames to produce topiary shapes.

1 *Canes secured together at the top to form a pyramid make an inexpensive and effective guide.*

2 *Trim back the excess growth until the plant is level with the guides.*

3 *Wire spheres look attractive even partially covered with foliage. Tie in shoots to encourage even coverage of the shape.*

❀ As always when pruning, check the individual needs of a particular plant before planning clipping. Clipping times will also depend on your local climate. In cooler climates, do not clip after early autumn as the young shoots produced will not be tolerant of low winter temperatures. Milder environments, in which the plants grow almost continuously, may necessitate regular clipping throughout the year. Most topiary plants should be clipped as thier summer growth begins, however, the exceptions to this are hornbeam and beech, which should not be clipped until the late summer.

SHAPING A HEDGE CORRECTLY

EFFECTIVE topiary needs even leaf coverage, which is hard to achieve on shapes that have a lot of leaf shade shielding the lower parts of the plant. Do not allow hedges to become top heavy, flat-topped or tapering towards the bottom, with a twiggy base. Slope the hedge from a narrow top to a wide base for greatest ease of pruning, healthy growth and an attractive appearance.

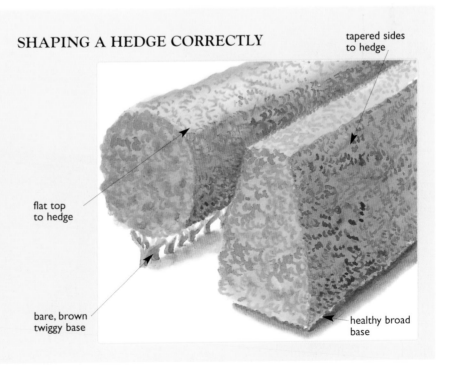

tapered sides to hedge

flat top to hedge

bare, brown twiggy base

healthy broad base

Acacia

Laurel

Bottle brush

Scotch heather

Camellia

PRUNING ORNAMENTAL PLANTS

GIVEN below are the pruning requirements of some popular plants, with advice on timing and the best method to employ to make the most of the plants.

Mimosa (*Acacia*)

✿ No regular pruning is required for mimosa except cutting back the dead wood after a severe winter. If you need to restrict the height of the shrub cut it right back to a third of its size following flowering.

Laurel (*Aucuba japonica*)

✿ No regular pruning is needed for laurel unless it grows beyond its allotted space, in which case it can be cut back in spring.

Bottle brush (*Callistemon*)

✿ No regular pruning is needed but it is sensible to thin out the old branches and shoots at the base of the plant from time to time.

Scotch heather, ling (*Calluna*)

✿ Heather quickly becomes straggly and untidy if left unpruned for any length of time. Luckily, it is easy to prune, merely requiring a quick clip over with shears in the early months of spring. Do not cut right back into the old wood, as bare patches will appear.

Camellia

✿ No hard pruning is required for camellias; any straggly shoots can be taken off following flowering in mid-spring. Deadheading on varieties with masses of blooms will increase growth for the following year.

Convolvulus

Dogwood

Convolvulvus

❀ To create a bushy appearance, remove about two thirds of this shrub annually in late summer. This will encourage new growth of the pretty silvery leaves and flowers the following year.

Dogwood (*Cornus*)

❀ Dogwoods grown for their coloured stems need pruning regularly to promote new growth. For winter colour, the stems should be cut right back to the basal level in late spring.

Daphne

Daphne

❀ No routine pruning is required for any of the many species of *Daphne*, but cut the straggly shoots out in early spring to keep a pleasing and neat appearance.

Bell heather *(Erica)*

❀ Clip off dead flowerheads to encourage new growth aand prune during the spring months when new growth is about to start.

Bell heather

Fuchsia magellanica

❀ The hardy fuchsia dies back in the winter as the top growth is killed by frost and low temperatures. Cut it right back almost to ground level in the spring and a profusion of new shoots will soon appear.

Fuchsia

Hebe

Helianthemum

Laburnum

Lace-cap hydrangea

Lavender

Shrubby veronica (*Hebe*)
✿ Some varieties of these plants are not very hardy and will need attention after the winter. Do not prune the plant until spring, even if the leaves are brown and the stems bare, as they offer some small protection against the elements. Cut the damaged shoots off when the new growth begins to appear and cut back for shape if needed after about a month.

Rock rose, sun rose (*Helianthemum*)
✿ Cut two-thirds of the new shoots in the summer months to encourage new growth the following year.

Tree hollyhock, Tree mallow (*Hibiscus*)
✿ Very little general maintenance is required for this hardy species. Remove old branches to restrict size and prune back any frost-damaged shoots in early spring.

Lace-cap hydrangea (*Hydrangea macrophylla*)
✿ Leave the dead brown heads on many varieties of hydrangea during the winter months to protect flower buds from damage. Instead, remove the dead heads in spring, when the weather is warmer and the first green shoots appear. Remove straggly shoots at the same time.

Laburnum
✿ As these plants grow so abundantly, train them into shape when they are young. If necessary, remove crossing or over-large branches in the later summer, but in general it is preferable not to prune them, as the wounds tend to bleed excessively.

Peony

Lupins

Lavender (*Lavundula*)

❀ Prune lavender to promote a neat appearance, since it can quickly become straggly and tatty. Cut right back to the new shoots in early spring as soon as the new shoots begin to appear. Keep lavender beds tidy by pruning them lightly with shears after flowering. Take cuttings for propagation in the summer.

Lupins (*Lupinus*)

❀ Lupins are short-term, fast-growing perennials that should be deadheaded after flowering to prevent reseeding. For bushy growth, cut one stem in three.

Cistaceae

Oleander (*Nerium*)

❀ Oleander is not a hardy plant and should be placed in a greenhouse in winter. Remove half of the year's new growth after the plant has flowered in early summer. As Oleander is poisonous, always wear protective gloves when pruning.

Peony (*Paeonia*)

❀ Remove all dead wood in mid-summer and cut off dead pieces of stem once the fruit-bearing shoots have died back.

Oleander

Rhododendron

❀ This spring-flowering shrub requires no regular pruning until it is fully grown, which takes around 10–15 years. At this point, cut one stem in every three in the summer to promote healthy growth and an attractive shape. Deadhead the flowers anually.

Rhododendron

PESTS AND WEEDS

You have planned and prepared your garden, planted your stock, and now you are beginning to anticipate a wonderful show of colour and texture that lasts throughout the year.

This is the point at which you are likely to become complacent – and this is when you very definitely must not! There are enemies lurking, and you must be vigilant if all your hard work is not to be ruined.

The dangers you may be up against include the elements, weeds – and a whole range of very determined bugs. Keeping an eye on the weather forecast will help you prepare for unexpected conditions such as storms or frosts, and regular weeding and mulching are essential.

When it comes to the bugs, however, one of the biggest challenges is to sort out which bugs are the unfriendly ones. This chapter gives you tips for managing these and other threats to your garden.

PLANT PROBLEMS AND WEED CONTROL

Viewed as a whole, this section can appear daunting – depressing even, with its litany of weeds, pests and diseases. However, with careful planting and garden maintenance there is no need to suppose that your garden will play host to all the ailments and problems listed here. Good-quality, healthy plants, given optimum growing conditions, will stand an excellent chance of resisting disease and throwing off pest problems. Practise careful hygiene and vigilant observation, so that you can tackle problems as soon as they occur.

PREVENTION

THE maxim 'prevention is better than cure' applies particularly to gardens. Increasingly, gardeners are turning away from the chemical control of problems, recognising that to rely on chemicals, for example in pesticides and fungicides, can create more problems than they cure. Helpful predators may be eradicated along with the pests, leading to an even worse pest problem.

❀ You may be a gardener who has diligently sprayed your garden against aphids for years, and wonder why, one long hot summer, your garden is plagued with aphids, while your neighbour's unsprayed plot is aphid free. The reason is that you have gradually wiped out the predators who are now so obligingly policing your neighbour's unsprayed garden. Of course, the wider global issues of pollution and the potential dangers from chemicals, as well as the matter of slowly destroying the ecosystem within your own garden, are also of concern when thinking about how to tackle plant problems.

Keeping problems in perspective

❀ The first thing to consider, before becoming hysterical about pests and diseases and automatically reaching for the nearest chemical spray, is to get matters into perspective. Some pests may be unsightly, but are actually not as hazardous to a plant as other threats, such as inclement weather. In fact, in general, weather issues are a much bigger risk to plant health than individual pests – something it is worth

ABOVE: *Some diseases, such as clubroot, can quickly affect an entire crop, so it is worth being vigilant about plant health.*

bearing in mind when you first spot a single caterpillar perched on your precious cabbages.

❀ The second biggest plant enemy is bad gardening practice. For example, overcrowding your plants leaves them prone to infection. Poor hygiene is another plant hazard. If you do not remove diseased material and burn, deeply bury or compost it well, you are inviting further plant troubles.

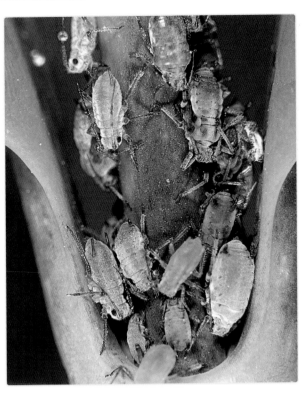

ABOVE: *A group of honeysuckle aphids cluster on the denuded axial of a leaf.*

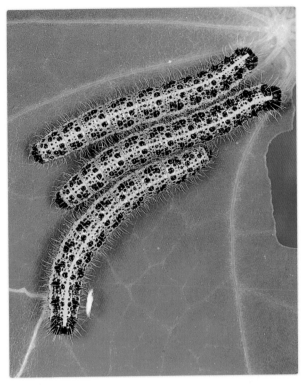

ABOVE: *Large white butterfly caterpillars, pictured on a damaged nasturtium leaf, are pests common to brassica crops and some ornamental plants.*

✤ This gives you some idea of the responsibility you have as a gardener. Your aim should be to maintain plant health, rather than allow problems to occur and get out of hand; and then curse the pests, who are in fact way down in the ranks of plant difficulties.

Minimising problems

✤ Keeping your garden healthy by careful and consistent adherence to gardening basics will go an enormous way towards preventing pests and diseases from overwhelming your plants. With the huge variety of plants on offer, it makes sense firstly to choose healthy looking specimens of disease-resistant strains, and plant them appropriately.

✤ A plant grown in the particular type of soil it needs, and where it can receive the amount of light it requires, has much more of a chance of surviving without problems than a plant grown without respect for its natural demands. Take care to provide the appropriate level of water, remembering that too much can be just as injurious as too little.

✤ Spacing is an important consideration. Plants grown too close together will compete for nutrients, and the

congested, humid conditions will encourage fungal disease. Follow the guidelines for optimum spacing that appear on individual plant labels.

✤ Garden hygiene is a factor often overlooked as being of serious concern in preventing problems. After all, muck is muck – at least visually. However, it is all too easy to transfer disease through poor hygiene, for example by planting in uncleaned pots, which may carry disease spores, or by propagating using a knife that has not been sterilised.

COMMON PESTS

THERE are a number of common pests that are a widespread problem for gardeners and attack a wide variety of plants.

Aphids

❀ Aphids are widely thought of as the ultimate garden scourge. They suck sap and excrete the excess as a sticky residue, which falls on foliage where it can turn mouldy. Emerging shoots and leaves can be damaged, and affected plants can become distorted and disfigured. Aphids can spread viral diseases between plants such as roses, lilies and tulips. Sooty mould often accompanies aphid attack, since the fungus lives on the 'honeydew' secreted by aphids.

❀ Ladybirds and hoverflies are the best organic control for aphids. Attract them by planting poached egg flowers (*Limnanthes douglasii*) and *Convolvulus tricolor*. Physically place ladybirds on affected leaves.

❀ Companion planting can help in other ways. You could plant sacrificial crops. For example, nasturtiums planted near broccoli are likely to suffer from aphid attack, leaving the broccoli clear. Chives deter aphids and are a pretty edging plant, making them an excellent choice for the herbaceous border.

❀ Spraying with a soft soap – not detergent – solution works well, too. In the greenhouse, parasitic controls are useful. In all cases, simply removing the aphids by hand is also effective and organically sound.

❀ The non-organic approach, possible on vulnerable non-food crops, uses selective systemic insecticides, which leaves beneficial insects unharmed.

Earwigs

❀ The distinctive pincers of the earwig are not generally seen during the day, since they feed at night. They shred the leaves and eat the flowers of plants such as dahlias, chrysanthemums and clematis. Earwigs are not all bad, however. They do eat quite a number of aphids, so if your plants are not being damaged, do not automatically operate a 'search and destroy' mission. To check whether earwigs are responsible for decimated flowers and leaves, investigate by torchlight.

❀ Inverted flowerpots, stuffed with straw and suspended on canes, will attract and trap earwigs, which can then be removed and disposed of.

Slugs and snails

❀ Slugs and snails attack many types of plant, including bulbs, herbaceous perennials, vegetables, strawberries,

ABOVE: *Earwigs shred the leaves of certain ornamental plants such as dahlias and can also attack food crops, but since they eat some aphids and codling moth eggs they are not generally considered a serious garden pest.*

ABOVE: *Aphids are a garden scourge, wreaking havoc on a wide variety of plants by damaging and distorting new leaves and shoots, as well as weakening the plant as a whole.*

ABOVE: *A shiny red lily beetle (Lilioceris lilii) on a damaged lily leaf.*

ABOVE: *An adult cock chafer (Melolontha melolontha) devours fresh green buds on a leaf.*

climbing plants and young seedlings. Although most live on top of the soil, some attack the underground parts of plants such as bulbs, as well as tubers like potatoes. Slugs and snails feed primarily at night or after rain.

✿ Some plants are particularly susceptible to slug and snail attack, such as hostas, delphiniums and all young seedlings. Plants known to be vulnerable should be protected with physical barriers, such as crushed eggshells, sawdust, wood ash or sharp sand.

✿ Slugs have sensitive skin and do not like crawling over these surfaces, but be aware that the barrier is only effective as long it is unbroken. Rain can easily break down these barriers, so either check regularly and replenish or choose a very effective (though not very attractive) barrier method – a ring 10 cm (4 in) high, cut from a plastic bottle and pushed 2.5 cm (1 in) into the ground.

✿ Slug 'pubs', containers of tempting fermenting beer sunk into the soil, are also a popular way of disposing of slugs without recourse to chemicals. However, these traps also drown beneficial creatures, unless you provide twiggy ladders in each one for ground beetles and the like.

✿ Inverted grapefruit skin halves are also used. The slugs congregate within, ready for you to dispose of as you see fit – either by removing them to a distant place, or drowning them. However, you will need quite a number of traps to catch the quantities of slugs that

congregate in most gardens, especially in moist conditions. Dedicated gardeners may be driven to seeking out slugs by torchlight, before giving them a burial at sea.

✿ Apart from mechanical and barrier methods, another organic option is a parasitic nematode, which can be watered on to the soil to kill slugs and snails.

✿ Methiocarb or metaldehyde slug pellets can affect animals higher up the food chain, such as birds and cats, and should be regarded as an absolute last resort. Aluminium sulphate pellets should harm only slugs and snails, but could leach aluminium salts into crops. Organic gardeners would not use these types of control.

BELOW: *Slugs are notoriously hard to eliminate but any effort to do so is worthwhile since, like snails, slugs cause damage not only to seedlings, but to all parts of a wide variety of mature plants.*

ABOVE: *Caterpillar damage on cabbage leaves.*

ABOVE: *This cabbage is displaying classic clubroot symptoms.*

Caterpillars and chafers

❀ There are many types of caterpillar, the most notorious of which is the caterpillar of the cabbage white butterfly. Caterpillars eat foliage, stems, flowers and fruits. Some caterpillars conceal themselves by curling up in young leaves or protecting themselves in a silk-like webbing, so if you see curled leaves and webbing, unroll them to investigate further. Leatherjackets are greyish-brown caterpillars, the larvae of crane flies. These soil-dwelling caterpillars eat the roots of young seedlings, immature plants and lawn grass.

❀ Remove any caterpillars by hand as soon as you notice them. There is an organically acceptable bacterial control, *Bacillus thuringiensis*, suitable for cabbage white caterpillar attacks. Alternatively, you can use special sticky bands of grease designed to prevent flightless pests like caterpillars climbing up the plants.

❀ Although, if left unchecked, caterpillars can munch their way unattractively through ornamentals, such as nasturtiums, as well as food crops like cabbages, the problem is not always critical. Nibbled leaves may look less than lovely, but often, only the external leaves are affected, the caterpillars having departed before the cabbage starts its main growth spurt.

PLANT DISEASES

THE general guidelines for good garden hygiene apply particularly to keeping disease at bay. Remove potential sources of infection by disinfecting pots, trays, canes and other equipment at the end of each season. Diligently remove and dispose of decaying, diseased or dead material by pruning out problem areas. Clear away plant debris that falls naturally, as these leaves and twigs may harbour fungal spores, which would reinfect plants the following spring.

❀ Practise crop rotation. This means not growing the same bedding plants or vegetables in the same spot each year. Overwintering pests and diseases emerge in spring to find that their target has vanished.

❀ Choose disease-resistant plant species where possible and plant them at the appropriate spacing. Keep the garden weed free, well watered and mulched.

Mildews

❀ These fungal diseases attack stressed plants, particularly those that have become dry at the roots and are in stagnant air conditions. Avoid overcrowding plants and keep them consistently watered and mulched in order to prevent this disease, which devours affected leaves and shoots from the outside. Downy mildew is more serious than powdery mildew, as it can penetrate the leaves and eventually kill the plant.

❀ Planting alliums in generous quantities near plants known to be susceptible to mildew is said to offer increased protection. Since alliums look spectacular paired with roses, this is a companion planting suggestion well worth trying but, as always, careful attention to spacing and watering of vulnerable plants is of prime importance.

❀ Remove affected areas to reduce the spread of mildew. There are some organic sprays available, such as those made of nettles or garlic, which claim to improve mildew resistance.

❀ The non-organic approach is to spray with a chemical fungicide, in addition to following the general guidelines on plant hygiene and care.

Grey mould *(botrytis)*

❀ Another fungal disease, which thrives in cool, damp conditions, *botrytis* is an unsightly grey mould, which covers leaves, stems and fruit. Poorly ventilated conditions, such as inside inadequately aired greenhouses or cloches, encourage the condition, as does overcrowding. Strawberries are particularly vulnerable to grey mould. Improve air flow and provide drier conditions to prevent and arrest the problem. Remove and destroy all affected parts of the plant.

❀ In addition to these measures, fungicides can also be used to control *botrytis* – there are organically acceptable ones available.

Rusts

❀ Rusts are a collection of fungal diseases that discolour leaves and encourage them to drop prematurely. They flourish in similar conditions to those that harbour mildews – that is, dank, overcrowded environments. Prevention guidelines are similar to those given for mildew. Take care to provide good ventilation and plant at appropriate spacings. Remove affected areas. Organically acceptable fungicides are available.

Wilts and rots

❀ Soil-dwelling organisms can cause plants to wilt – particularly chrysanthemums, clematis, tomatoes and carnations. Good plant hygiene and garden husbandry will help prevent wilt, which affects weak and generally unhealthy plants. Use fresh, sterile compost for seeds and cuttings, as wilt often attacks new seedlings. In the border, incorporating good quality garden compost will help plant health as the beneficial organisms it contains will help control any bad ones.

COMMON PLANT DISORDERS

1. *Uneven germination caused by damping off in lobelia seedlings.*

2. *A shot hole caused by bacterial canker on cherry leaves.*

3. *A viral disease on a* Pelargonium, *causing leaf venation.*

4. *Coral spot fungal fruiting bodies on the dying wood of an ornamental tree mallow.*

5. *Grey mould damage on the leaves of a* Pelargonium *plant.*

6. *Powdery mildew affecting the foliage of Achillea ptarmica 'The Pearl' in late flowering.*

7. *Close-up of the underside of a rose leaf, showing black teliospore pustules.*

PLANT DISORDERS

SOME plants may appear to have suffered pest or disease damage, but are actually displaying signs of nutritional deficiency or a physiological disorder. Common sense plant care will go a long way towards preventing these problems. For example, planting an acid-loving plant such as an azalea in a heavily alkaline soil is not going to produce a happy, healthy plant, unless the soil local to the plant is regularly adapted to its needs. Such a plant, grown in an alkaline soil, would show stunted growth and yellowing leaves, the symptoms of lime-induced chlorosis (manganese/iron deficiency). Protecting plants from weather damage, be it frost or drought, is also a basic element of garden practice that will give your plants the best possible chance of healthy growth. You will do well to learn to recognise the common plant disorders.

Nitrogen deficiency

❀ Pale green plants that eventually turn yellow, with weak, thin, pinkish-coloured stems and stunted growing tips can indicate a nitrogen deficiency. Older leaves turn yellowish-red along the veins and die off. The whole plant will have its growth checked and generally become spindly and unhealthy looking. Growing plants in restricted conditions where they are inadequately fed, or in poor, light soil can cause nitrogen deficiency. This is the commonest plant disorder as nitrogen is so readily leached out of the soil. Make sure your plants have a soil that is adequately fertile, regularly dressed with well-rotted manure and balanced fertilisers. As an emergency remedy where deficiency has been noticed, a high-nitrogen fertiliser or liquid feed can be applied.

Waterlogging

❀ When plant roots suffer a lack of oxygen, the plant becomes waterlogged (unless it is a bog plant). Although there is obviously plenty of water, the plant will wilt as if it was being under watered and its leaves will yellow. If you lift the plant, you may see black, even rotten roots, as the plant starts to die back. To prevent this condition, provide adequate drainage by regularly digging in plenty of organic matter to improve the soil structure. If the problem occurs in containers, there may be inadequate drainage holes, or they may have become clogged with debris. If you have localised areas in the garden that are particularly prone to waterlogging, then you might want to consider growing plants in raised beds. If the problem is more widespread, consider installing drainage pipes, or grow plants suited to boggy conditions.

ABOVE: *Potato plants, showing the effects of drought in a dried-up vegetable patch.*

ABOVE: *The effects of leaf scorch on daffodil plants, causing fused leaves and flowers.*

Drought

❀ When plants suffer a prolonged water shortage, they wilt and collapse, with dried out, curling leaves. Eventually, the plant will die. Container-grown plants are especially vulnerable, as are young plants on light soils. To reduce the potential for drought damage, incorporate plenty of well-rotted organic matter into the soil, and add water-retaining granules to containers. Water really adequately each time, rather than watering little and often, as this can lead to surface rooting, which will only aggravate the problem.

Frost damage

❀ Frost damage is sickeningly familiar to many gardeners. The blackened, dying remains of what was fresh new growth all too often serve as a reminder of how a late spring frost can take the gardener, and the vulnerable young plants newly planted out, unawares. In especially cruel frosts, even woody plants can split their stems. Almost any plant can suffer from frost damage if conditions are harsh enough – even plants that are generally accepted as being hardy. If particularly low temperatures are anticipated (below 0°C/32°F), protect vulnerable plants using fleece, cloches or cold frames.

If you live in an area where frosts are common, plant accordingly, using plants that can usually survive in harsh weather conditions.

Manganese/iron deficiency

❀ This deficiency is commonly seen where lime-hating plants such as camellias or rhododendrons have been grown in a very alkaline soil. The leaf veins remain green, but the rest of the leaf turns pale and yellow, and the leaves may brown along the edges. The plant will generally have checked growth and will fail to thrive. The simplest form of prevention is to plant according to the particular soil requirements of a species. If you have a burning desire to grow a plant that would not do well in your garden soil, then restrict yourself to growing it in a container, where you can provide the acidic conditions it needs, using ericaceous compost. If beds or borders are showing this deficiency, you could correct it in the short term using sequestered iron. In the longer term, apply good-quality compost and well-rotted manure regularly.

ABOVE: *Very cold weather can cause damage to vulnerable plants. Protect precious specimens and knock heavy falls of snow off plants before it freezes.*

ABOVE: *The tell-tale symptoms of manganese deficiency showing on a rose leaf.*

WEED CONTROL

WEEDS are simply plants growing in the wrong place. This is worth remembering before you automatically reach for the weed killer or scythe. Some plants are considered weeds by one gardener, who works hard to eradicate them, yet are admired by another, who may propagate them from seed, or buy them as fully grown plants at the garden centre. Mind-your-own-business (*Helxine soleirolii*) and poppies (*Papaver*), for example, are plants that can be viewed as attractive, desirable cultivars or irritatingly pervasive weeds, depending on their location and the preference of the individual gardener. Mind-your-own-business can enliven dull paving with its lush, low-growing green carpeting effect, but can wreak havoc in what is meant to be a perfect lawn.

❀ The organic gardener appreciates the value of weeds as free sources of fertility, and works with weeds, rather than directly against them. Weeds are mineral accumulators, rendering minerals accessible to crops. For example, nettles accumulate potassium. Nettles have many other useful attributes, particularly in association with fruit and vegetables. In a large garden the keen organic gardener will find an appropriate place to give over to nettle growing – as good companions for plants such as redcurrants and blackberries, as hosts to many species of butterfly and to make into nettle sprays, which protect leeks from leek flies and moths.

❀ These positive attributes aside, good weed control undoubtedly has a vital role to play in maintaining a healthy garden. Weeds compete with desirable plants for nutrients, water and light, and can play host to diseases, which can spread to other plants. For example, groundsel often harbours greenfly, mildew and rust. Weeds are often extremely tough and pernicious, and can quickly colonise cultivated areas if left untamed.

Annual weeds

❀ Common annual weeds include groundsel, chickweed, nipplewort, shepherd's purse, annual nettle.

❀ Annual weeds grow from seed when the soil is moist, warm and exposed to light, thus mulching (covering the soil in order to block out the light, as well as for other reasons) or deep burying will prevent germination of annual weeds.

❀ Hoeing is often recommended as a control for annual weeds. The roots are severed from the stems to prevent further development. Walk backwards when hoeing, so that you do not tread the weeds into the soil. Hoe before the weeds have set seed. Allowed to germinate, the resulting weeds are quite easy to kill, but if left unchecked they can become more resilient.

Perennial weeds

❀ Common perennial weeds include ground elder, bindweed, dandelion, stinging nettle, horsetail.

❀ Mulching is less effective at controlling perennial weeds. Many perennial weeds such as dandelions have long, fleshy roots, which ensure the survival of the plant even if the top growth is killed off. These weeds will need to be dug out entirely. Some will regenerate if even a tiny portion of the root is left in the soil. Systemic weed killers are often used to control perennial weeds – particularly those that are very difficult to dig out completely, such as horsetail, which can develop roots that grow to depths of at least 1.8 m (6 ft). When a system weed killer is applied to leaves and stems, it is gradually absorbed by the weed and transported through the entire plant via the sap, eventually killing the whole weed.

ABOVE: *Regular hoeing is an efficient way of controlling annual weeds.*

Mulching for weed control

❀ Covering the soil around desirable plants with material that blocks out light and moisture has grown in popularity as a way of controlling weeds without recourse to chemicals.

❀ Although organic mulches have the added benefits of improving soil fertility and structure, they are not as effective as inorganic mulches at suppressing weed growth. Organic mulches need to be at least 10 cm (4 in) deep in order to be effective. Black plastic, however, is a very effective weed-suppressing mulch. Simply cut a cross in the plastic and plant desirable specimens through it. Conceal the unattractive plastic with bark or gravel.

Planting ground cover for weed control

❀ Ground cover plants will help keep weeds down by competing with them. However, they will not win the battle unless they are given a head start, by being planted in weed-free soil in sites suited to their individual needs. Planting ground cover through a plastic mulch, and concealing the plastic with gravel or bark, is an excellent and attractive way to keep weeds to a minimum.

❀ Good ground cover plants include periwinkle (*Vinca*) and lady's mantle (*Alchemilla mollis*).

COMMON GARDEN WEEDS

1. *Young nipplewort plant.*

2. *Annual nettle plant in flower.*

3. *Groundsel in flower.*

4. *Thistle in full bloom.*

5. *Flowering dandelion in grass.*

6. *Bindweed choking other plants.*

7. *Young ground elder plant.*

8. *Field buttercups in full flower.*

INDEX

Italic page numbers refer to illustrations.

A
Acacia 80, 80
acid soil 25, 41
acid-loving plants 92
Ailanthus 66
air layering 62
alkaline soil 25
alliums 90
anvil secateurs 13
aphids 86, 87, 88, 88
arches 75
Aucuba japonica 80, 80
automated watering 31
autumn daffodil 60

B
bark 39
beech 79
bell heather 81, 81
biological control 88, 89, 90
black plastic 40, 95
Botrytis 91
bottle brush 80, 80
box 78
broadcast sowing 52, 53
buddleja 68
bulb division 60–1
bulblets 60, 61
bypass secateurs 13

C
cacti 23
Callistemon 80, 80
Calluna 80, 80
camellias 80, 80, 93
caterpillars 86, 87, 90
chafers 89, 90
chives 88
clay soil 24, 25
clematis 70, 74–5
climate 20–3, 79
climbers 70–1, 74–5
climbing roses 72, 73
cocoa shells 40
cold frames 44, 46, 47, 47
companion planting 88, 90
compost 26, 48
compost bins 26, 27
containers
    feeding 33
    watering 30–1
Convolvulus 81, 81
    C. tricolor 88
coppicing 68
cormlets 60
corms 60
Cornus 69, 81, 81
Cotinus coggygria 62
crocuses 60
crop rotation 90
cuttings 48, 54–7
cuttings compost 48
cyclamens 60

D
damping off 48, 50
Daphne 81, 81

deadheading 69, 72
deciduous trees 66
delphiniums 89
dieback 64
digging 29, 34–7
disease 64, 86–7, 90–1
division 58–61
dogwoods 65, 69, 81, 81
double digging 29, 35, 37
drainage 28–9
drill sowing 52, 53
drip-feed systems 31
drought 22–3, 92, 93
Dutch hoe 12

E
earwigs 88, 88
Egyptians 11
equipment 10–19
Erica 81, 81
evergreen trees 66

F
feeding 32–3
fertilisers 32–3, 41
fibre fleece 40
firming in 50
floribunda roses 73
forks 10–12, 36–7
formative pruning 65
French drain 29
French layering 62
frost 21, 93
frost pockets 22
fruit 65
Fuchsia magellanica 81, 81

G
gloves 17
gravel 41
Grecian saw 14
greenhouses 46
grey mould 91
grit 41
ground cover 95

H
hand forks 12
Hanging Gardens
    of Babylon 11
hardening off 51
hardwood 18
hardwood cuttings 54, 57
heather 69, 80, 80, 81, 81
Hebe 82, 82
Hedera helix 62, 62
hedges 76–7, 79
heel cuttings 56
Helianthemum 82, 82
Helxine soleirolii 94
herbs 78
Hibiscus 82
hoes 12, 94
honeysuckle 70, 70
hornbeam 79
hoses 14, 30, 31
hostas 89
humidity 21
humus 26, 29, 32, 41
hybrid tea roses 73

Hydrangea 68
    H. macrophylla 82, 82
hygiene 45, 48, 55, 86, 87, 90

I
inorganic fertilisers 32
inorganic mulches 40–1
inorganic soil improvers 27
iron deficiency 93
ivy 62, 62, 70

K
kneeling frames 15
kneeling mats 15
knives 12

L
laburnum 82, 82
lace-cap hydrangea 82, 82
laurel 78, 80, 80
Lavandula 69, 82, 83
lavender 69, 82, 83
lawn edging tools 16
lawn rakes 12
lawnmowers 15
layering 62–3
leaf mould 26
leatherjackets 90
lilies 60, 61
lime 27, 41
Limnanthes douglasii 88
ling 80, 80
loam 24
local climate 20
loppers 13
lupins 24, 83, 83

M
manganese deficiency 93, 93
manufactured board 18
manure 40
microclimate 20
mildew 90
mimosa 80, 80
mind-your-own business 94
miniature roses 72
mist propagators 47
mulberry tree 66
mulches 30, 38–41, 94, 95

N
narcissi 60
nasturtiums 88
natural layering 62
Nerium 83, 83
nettles 94
nitrogen 32
    deficiency 92

O
oleander 83, 83
organic fertilisers 32
organic gardening 94
organic matter 26, 29, 30, 41
organic mulches 39–40
organic soil improvers 26
ornamental trees 67

P
Papaver 94

parrot-beak secateurs 13
pebbles 41
peony 83, 83
perennials, division 59
pergolas 18, 18, 75
pesticides 86
pests 84–95
phosphorus 32
planning 28
plant foods 32–3
poached egg flower 88
pollarding 68
poppies 94
potassium 32
potting on 52
power trimmers 76, 77
preservatives 18–19
pricking out 50, 51
privet 76
propagation 44–63
propagators 44, 45, 46–7
pruning 64–83
pruning saws 14, 68

R
railway sleepers 18
rainfall 22–3
raised beds 20
rakes 12
rambling roses 72
ratchet secateurs 13
red lily beetle 89
regenerative pruning 65, 72
renovative pruning 64–5,
71, 77
residual current device 17,
47, 76
rhizomes 58, 59
rhododendrons 83, 83, 93
rock rose 82, 82
roses 65, 72–3, 90
rots 91
rusts 91

S
safety 16–17, 76
sandy soil 24, 25, 37
saws 14
scaling bulbs 61
Scarborough lilies 60
scoring bulbs 61
Scotch heather 80, 80
seaside gardens 23
secateurs 13, 77, 78
seed compost 48
seed trays 45, 49
seedbeds 52
seedlings 50–1, 53, 89
seeds see sowing
seep hoses 31
semi-ripe cuttings 54, 56
serpentine layering 62
shears 13, 77, 78
shrub roses 72
shrubby veronica 82, 82
shrubs, pruning 69–70
silty soil 24, 25
simple digging 35
simple layering 62
single digging 35, 36

slugs and snails 87, 88–9, 89
smoke bush 62
snowberry 76
snowdrops 60
softwood 18
softwood cuttings 54, 55
soil
    conditioners 32
    improvement 26–7
    pH 25, 41
    structure 24–5
    texture 25
    types 24
    warming cables 47
sowing
    indoors 48–52
    outdoors 44, 52–3
    in trays 49
spades 10–11, 34–5, 36–7
stem-tip cuttings 54, 55
Sternbergia 60
stool layering 62
storage, tools 17
strawberries 62
strimmers 16
subsoil 24, 37
suckers 73
sun rose 82, 82

T
temperature 21
thinning out 53
tip layering 62
tools 10–19
top dressing 38–41
topiary 13, 78–9
topsoil 24, 37
tree of heaven 66
tree hollyhock 82
tree mallow 82
tree pruners 13
trees, pruning 66–8
trench layering 62
trimmers 16
trowels 12

V
Vallota 60
variegated plants 64–5

W
water-retaining gel 30–1
watering 30–1, 50, 52
watering cans 15, 31
waterlogging 92
weeds 94–5
wheelbarrows 14
willows 65
wilts 91
wind 23
windbreaks 23
wood treatment 18–19
wounding 56

Y
yew 78